A WORLD WITHIN

Jewish Life as Reflected in Muslim Court Documents from the *Sijill* of Jerusalem

(XVIth Century)

PART ONE

(Texts)

AMNON COHEN

A Jewish Quarterly Review Supplement: 1994

"Truth is often very improbable, and factual evidence can only in small measure be replaced by deductions and speculations."

(Sigmund Freud, from an unpublished introduction to *Moses and Monotheism*, as cited by Y. H. Yerushalmi, *Freud's Moses: Judaism Terminable and Interminable*, 1991, p. 17).

PREFACE

The Story behind the Story

The Six Day War was a watershed in the history of the Middle East and the people living there. Best known for the major military events and equally important political and socio-economic changes it brought about, that war also changed many major perspectives of academic research pertaining to the Middle East, my own included.

In spite of my heritage–perhaps because of it–I had never intended to conduct any research on Jews. The focus of my studies had always been Arabs and Turks, i.e. Muslims, rather than Jews. Nor did I ever seriously think Jerusalem was a "promised land" where authentic historical data on the Ottoman Empire could be sought and found. In the earlier stages of my academic career I discovered to my dismay that the few documents on Ottoman Palestine that had survived when the Republic of Turkey inherited the Ottoman Empire, were to be found either in Istanbul or in various European archives, rather than in Jerusalem.

"The Opening of East Jerusalem," to paraphrase the title of a well-known book in our field, brought about a complete change in my own perspective of research; in a wider context, however, it turned out to be most conducive to modern historical research relating to that particular part of the world. The vaults of many monasteries in the Old City contained historical treasures in more than one sense of the word. Documents pertaining to Greek-Orthodox or Armenian communal history in Jerusalem were not immediately put on public display, but gradually became accessible to those scholars who were both persistent and fortunate in pursuing and eventually acquiring the support of the usually reluctant and still highly suspicious custodians of the respective archives. Natural caution, and perhaps more than a modicum of intellectual envy and fancied competition, continued to play a major role in the stubborn objection of these custodians to any attempt to share the untapped sources at their disposal with the international community of scholars. Practically nothing of a Jewish nature was left on the surface of the land that had now become accessible, other than some material relics in the shape of old tombstones or dilapidated walls, and those almost immediately became the scenes of archeological excavations. Islam, the third monotheistic religion, left the most numerous–and qualitatively the most impressive–marks on Jerusalem's grounds. Quite naturally, therefore, historians of architecture and art focused on aspects of the Muslim past of Jerusalem.[1]

For students of Muslim history, and of Ottoman history in particular, the documents stored in the archives of the *sharī'a* religious court of Jerusalem (commonly known as the *sijill*) were looked upon as the crown jewel. At the time no one knew of the Mamluk kadi's cache which included approximately 900 documents of the late 14th century;[2] it would be found later by the curator of the Islamic Museum on the Temple Mount. Some of us, however, were acquainted with the small number of earlier references to a huge body of documents in Jerusalem dating from the following 400 years of Ottoman rule.[3] The question confronting us was: Had these archives survived the war, and if so, how could we possibly gain access to them?

I did not know where to look for the archives. Moreover, I was not sure whether a search would be advisable. I consulted experienced archivists who agreed that the worst course would be to initiate a search that might alarm those in charge of the *sijill* archives. The consequence might then be the relocation of the records across the border to Jordan. Therefore, I did not follow my initial impulse but refrained from taking even preliminary steps that might create unnecessary tension. About three years later, at the Foreign Ministry library in Jerusalem, I came across a lengthy article in the Egyptian

---

[1] Michael H. Burgoyne, *Mamluk Jerusalem: An Architectural Study* (London, 1987).

[2] Donald P. Little, *A Catalogue of the Islamic Documents from al-Ḥaram aš-Šarīf in Jerusalem* (Beirut, 1984).

[3] Jon E. Mandaville "The Ottoman Court Records of Syria and Jordan," *Journal of the American Oriental Society* 86 (1966): 311-319.

newspaper *al-Ahrām*, where *shaykh* 'Abd al-Ḥamīd al-Sā'iḥ, the former Chief kadi and head of the religious administration of Jerusalem, castigated the Israeli authorities for a variety of alleged "desecrations" of Muslim holy sites which–according to him–called for immediate international intervention. In this article he referred specifically to the *sijill* archives of Jerusalem. Neither UNESCO nor any other international agency (otherwise quite aggressive in monitoring Israeli activities in Jerusalem) had ever involved themselves in this matter which was purely a figment of the distinguished writer's imagination. But for me these were sufficient grounds to stop hesitating and begin my search. If in any case Israel was being blamed for mishandling the archives, no attempt of mine to find them could be interpreted as tampering with a sensitive issue and causing an unwarranted problem.

When I approached the heads of the Higher Muslim Council, the late *shaykh* Ḥilmī al-Muḥtasib and the kadi of Jerusalem, *shaykh* Sa'īd Ṣabrī, I was asked to submit a written application which would be presented to their respective institutions, as well as to the Jordanian authorities in Amman. After several weeks of intensive deliberations, they granted me permission to conduct my research at the very heart of the Muslim presence and authority in East Jerusalem–the offices of the *waqf* administration and the Higher Muslim Council. Once the staff overcame their initial reticence, I received a most friendly welcome, and gradually became almost a permanent fixture in the huge court hall. For several years, until joined by some of my former students and current colleagues,[4] I was the only foreign researcher there. We were always aware of the sensitivity to our presence: we were looked upon as representing a foreign, even an adversarial, religion and we shared space with the local staff in the midst of a highly charged political conflict between our two communities. Sometimes we had to bear the brunt of an immediate political crisis or an unjustified measure taken by an emotionally motivated official, but we could always turn to and count on the help of the highest religious authority in Muslim Jerusalem, *shaykh* Sa'd al-Dīn al-'Alamī. He would always step in, and, after learning the facts, apply his vast experience and astute political judgment to resolve whatever problem arose, and enable us to continue our research. I knew that, political controversy notwithstanding, in our case the venerated *shaykh* could be relied upon to apply the age-old Muslim ideal of "the search of knowledge" (*ṭalab al-'ilm*) that should always be upheld and promoted.

The archives (to which physical access was prohibited, requested volumes being brought to the reading-hall) proved to be much larger in size and richer in authentic documents than even professional historians could have guessed. There are 420 leather-bound volumes, hardly touched by foreign or local scholars. The Turkish language volumes were not even paginated (we were asked by the court authorities to number each page). Over the years, above all during

[4] Amy Singer, *Palestinian Peasants and Ottoman Officials: Rural Administration around Sixteenth-Century Jerusalem* (Cambridge, U.K, 1994); 'Adel Manna', "The *Sijill* as Source for the Study of Palestine during the Ottoman Period, with Special Reference to the French Invasion" in *Palestine in the Late Ottoman Period: Political, Social and Economic Transformation*, ed. D. Kushner (Jerusalem and Leiden, 1986), pp. 351-362.

the 19th century, the size of these volumes varied, but all those that were compiled during the 16th century are basically identical: Of the 82 volumes for the 16th century, 66 were written in Arabic on pages measuring 28 x 21 cm; 16 volumes of Turkish documents were copied on the same size paper which was then folded in the middle; hence these volumes measure 28 x 10.5 cm.

The *sijill* documents were originally kept separately by the court and throughout the centuries were stored near one of the gates of the Temple Mount (*Bāb al-Nāẓir* in earlier years, *Bāb al-Silsila* later) in a building where the court convened regularly. Some time during World War II all of these volumes were leather bound, and several years later they were transferred to the newly established offices of the administration of the *waqf* on East Jerusalem's main street, Ṣalāḥ al-Dīn. Although the main purpose of the bindings was to better preserve this precious collection, and in themselves the bindings are very impressive, substantial damage to parts of these volumes resulted from poor workmanship. The use of wide scotch-tape, which was intended to reinforce the bindings, has lost some of its transparency over the years. Hence the blurred margins of many facsimiles. The inferior quality of other facsimiles resulted from either imprecise measurement of light or poor focusing by the photographers of the court archives, while operating the very sophisticated professional photographic equipment at their disposal. In some cases the poor quality of the reproduction stemmed from the poor grade of paper or ink used by the local Ottoman scribe at the time. Parts of the verso of some document pages actually show through on the recto side of the reproductions.

Actually, all these documents are drafts of court cases. The final decisions were given or sent to the litigants; hence there is often reference to "its writer" (*kātibuhu)*, usually the court scribe who penned the original document. A rare confirmation of the fact that these *sijill*s were regarded as copies, and not originals, is provided in volume 55, page 172 (a), (see below): a kadi (very likely a junior one) is referred to as "the writer of its original" (*kātib aṣlihi*), i.e. the authentic document describing the case and quite often reporting the decision reached by the judge, the copy of which was made in the *sijill* series, which remained in the court. Since in the course of time the original documents have disappeared, this procedure of routinely keeping copies of all court cases has provided us the only source for the text as the judge originally dictated it to the scribe.

The volumes are arranged chronologically, i.e. the court scribe (*kātib*) would copy the daily proceedings, indicating at the outset both the date and day of the week. Each document (usually referred to in Arabic by the same term, *sijill*) however, also bears a date at the end, and this is not superfluous since documents were often copied at the court long after the original day of litigation. As a result the material in the entire series is not organized by topic.[5] Since headings are usually not provided, the task of identifying *sijill* elements containing a common topic is far from easy. This problem is compounded when we bear in mind that each page includes several cases, and the average volume, usually covering approximately one year, contains some 450 pages. Jewish matters, therefore, were not

---

[5] The only two exceptions for the 16th century were volume 50 (dealing with inheritances) and volume 70 (*defter-i mufaṣṣal*).

easy to identify. Arabic script, unfortunately, does not have capital letters, a characteristic which would have made attempts at "spotting" easier. Cases involving Jewish litigants were copied like all others, in the chronological order of their appearance in court, and therefore do not emerge in a pre-set order. Haphazardly copied, they have nothing in form or substance to set them apart from the multitude of "regular" cases that involved only Muslims.

Cases concerning Jews cover a very wide spectrum of topics. If we bear in mind that the Jews of Jerusalem had their own separate courts, the number of cases brought to the Muslim court (which actually meant putting themselves at the mercy of a judge outside the pale of their communal and religious identity) is quite impressive. The present study totaling about 1000 entries, is an accumulation of most "Jewish" cases found in the 16th-century registers. The first part of this work presents a summary of each of those cases. The second part contains facsimiles of the relevant documents reproduced in identical order, reduced by approximately 20 percent. References in the two parts of this book are as follows: the volume number appears to the left of the slash, the page number to its right, followed by a letter indicating the location of the relevant document on the page, e.g. 20/315(a) means volume 20, p. 315, first entry. Most of these documents are written in Arabic, indicating how small an inroad was made by the Turkish language in the recently conquered Arabic speaking provinces. There was almost no significant infusion of Turkish words into the local vernacular of Jerusalem in the 16th century, and even less, in formal texts. Wherever the original document was written in Turkish, a special reference to that effect has been added in both parts of the book.

These *sijills* were initially not intended to be used for any purpose other than for the court's future reference. Hence the difficulty of deciphering the various handwritings that sometimes were sloppy, at other times, almost illegible. This also meant that they were unedited and unadulterated as the reader of the facsimiles can easily see; we tried to preserve some of this quality in our summaries as well. The English rendering of all technical terms (administrative titles, weights and measurements, coins etc.) is followed by their original Arabic or Turkish forms, and all personal names have been transcribed exactly as they appeared in the original. By doing so we not only avoided interpretative pitfalls but in many cases acquired unexpected insights into the original pronunciation of these words.[6] We avoided "correcting" a scribe's errors when refering to things Jewish, particularly in cases where personal names were cited, even when the Hebrew original form was readily identifiable (hence Hayin was not rendered Ḥayim, nor was Fraym replaced by the doubtless correct Hebrew Efrayim). Family names hardly existed in 16th-century Ottoman Jerusalem; a person was referred to by his or her first name followed by the father's name. The latter relationship was indicated by the Arabic equivalent for "the son of" (*ibn*) or "the daughter of" (*bint*), both of which we rendered "b." for the sake of brevity. Dates were also left in their authentic form, i.e. according to the *hijrī*

[6] The best example for this is provided in those cases where the scribe scrupulously copied the Hebrew word he heard, preserving even the Ashkenazi pronunciation (*qūshīr* and *ṭrayf*), see below, volume 12 page 263.

calendar,[7] but the heading of every volume was followed by the equivalent year or two according to the Gregorian calendar which is more familiar to the modern reader.

Over the years I have published a variety of books and articles based predominantly on these archives.[8] The documents themselves, however, remained almost unavailable to scholars; much of the rich information they contain therefore is virtually as inaccessible for research today as it was years ago. For those who subscribe to the old-fashioned ideals of an open, unlimited and unhampered search for truth, there was a clear obligation to make these historical documents available to the widest possible circle of scholars. In the context of Jewish history, this obligation was felt even more strongly. The difficult court circumstances and the burden of Middle Eastern

---

[7] Cf. Wolsley Haig, *Comparative Tables of Muhammadan and Christian Dates* (London, 1932).

[8] *Jewish Life under Islam* (Cambridge MA: Harvard University Press, 1984); *Economic Life in Ottoman Jerusalem* (Cambridge UK: Cambridge University Press, 1989); "Gold and Silver Crafting in Ottoman Jerusalem: The Role Played by the Guild," *Tārīḫ* 1 (Philadelphia: Annenberg Research Institute, 1990): 55-67; "Le Rouge et le Noir - Jerusalem Style" in *Villes au Levant, hommage a André Raymond, Revue du monde musulman et de la mediterranée*, No. 55/56 (Aix-en-Provence, 1990), pp. 141-151; "The Walls of Jerusalem" in *The Islamic World, from Classical to Modern Times: Essays in Honor of Bernard Lewis*, ed. C.E. Bosworth, Charles Issawi, R. Savory, and A. L. Udovitch, (Princeton: The Darwin Press, 1989), pp. 467-477; "Ritual Murder Accusations against the Jews during the Days of Suleiman the Magnificent" *Journal of Turkish Studies, Raiyyet Rusumu, Essays presented to Halil Inalcik* (Cambridge, MA: Harvard University Press, 1986), vol. 10, pp. 73-78; "Ottoman Rule and the Re-emergence of the Coast of Palestine (17th-18th centuries)," *Revue de l'occident musulman et de la mediterranée, les Ottomans en Mediterranée* 39 (Aix-en-Provence, 1985), pp. 163-175; "Sixteenth Century Egypt and Palestine: The Jewish Connection as Reflected in the Sijill of Jerusalem" in *Egypt and Palestine, a Millenium of Association*, ed. A. Cohen and G. Baer (New York: St. Martin's Press, 1984), pp. 232-240. I also published several Hebrew articles and books, most recently (with Elisheva Simon-Pikali) *Jews in the Moslem Religious Court* (Jerusalem: Yad Ben-Zvi, 1993).

politics made the objectively onerous task of deciphering and comprehending these documents that much harder.

When Bernard Lewis accepted the directorship of the Annenberg Research Institute in Philadelphia in 1986 he not only created an exemplary center for the conduct of scholarly research in Judaic and Near Eastern studies, but also undertook several far-sighted documentation projects, including this work. In spite of changing agendas, other directors of the Institute have generously supported my efforts and enabled me, as a fellow at the recently renamed Center for Judaic Studies of the University of Pennsylvania, to bring this project to its culmination during the academic year 1993/1994. I would like to express my gratitude to David Goldenberg and the entire staff of the Center for the unstinting help that made the realization of this book possible. Special thanks to Etty Lassman who did not hesitate to remind me constantly that she had other fellows to attend to, but with equal perseverance introduced me to the secrets of the proper use of the Macintosh computer, and was helpful far beyond the call of duty in bringing this project to an end. Last but not least, I thank the indefatigable Shirley Shpira in Jerusalem for seeing me through the labyrinthine maze of the English language in this work, as well as in all my other literary endeavors.

INTRODUCTION

A World Apart?

The Jews of Jerusalem were regarded by both their Arab neighbors and their Turkish masters as special beings. This manifested itself in a variety of ways. They were not only referred to by special terms such as *yahūd,* or *yahūdīler* (Arabic and Turkish, respectively), but technically were designated as a separate category, as *ṭā'ifa* or *ṭā'ife*, i.e. "a class, sect, body of men; a nation" (to use the translation of James W. Redhouse in his *Turkish and English Lexicon*). In the historical context of the 16th century the last word suggested by Redhouse may seem somewhat anachronistic, but the concept it indicates is basically correct–the Jews are viewed as a separate category and entity. The use of the adjective "Jewish" to describe a neighborhood they chose to live in conveys a sense of uniqueness to their place of residence,[9] over and above their appearance and religious difference. That the Jews were regarded as essentially different from the majority was best epitomized by the administrative provision that their affairs be conducted by a "head of the community of Jews" (*shaykh al-yahūd*). As the "head" he regulated–along with other community leaders–not only internal community matters but all dealings with the authorities, whether

[9] It was not exclusively Jewish, but a Jewish quarter within a Muslim neighborhood. Cf. my *Jewish Life*, pp. 17-20, 206-209.

financial, economic, or linked to their particular ritualistic-religious precepts.

These definitions, although seemingly derived from a theoretical analysis, are actually taken from the first volume of the *sijill* entries summarized on pages 24-25 below. Although these cases were grouped at random in one volume, they readily lend themselves to a much wider interpretation from which the reader can draw a multifaceted picture of Jewish life in Jerusalem at that time. If we visualize all these cases as dots on an imaginary drawing–dots vaguely appearing and disappearing among the vast number of legal cases involving the Muslim majority–and sketch a line linking all these dots together, we shall actually be reconstructing the special traits of Jewish life in Ottoman Jerusalem. On the other hand, the very same legal cases may also be looked upon as a mirror image of the historical picture, viz. Jewish involvement in the local affairs of the Muslim population.

Reality was much more diverse and encompassed many more facets than those which came to the attention of the court and are reported in volume 1, but even these cases amply document the "normal" character of Jewish life in Jerusalem. By definition, Jewish dietary laws dictated certain economic activities: Jews had to slaughter their own meat, leading to an elaborate set of rules and regulations as to when, where, and how these activities should be performed by the Jewish members of the butchers guild. As expected, Jews lent money to their needy coreligionists. But Jewish economic activities were much more impressive both in size and quality. Involvement in money matters was of an open-ended nature:

Jews lent money to Muslims (and occasionally to Christians) and borrowed money from them. As money changers, they were among the fiscal pillars of the local economy and provided the local population with the kinds of coins prescribed by the central administration. They also contributed regularly to the financial needs of specific Muslim endowments. Their economic transactions with members of the Muslim military establishment (e.g. the purchase of milling equipment) indicate a wider scope of both social and economic involvement within the local milieu. These few examples serve to point to another major finding provided by these documents–i.e. there was massive Jewish participation in organized professional activity. Contrary to earlier assertions,[10] we now know that the guild system was alive and intensely operative in Jerusalem at the time, and it encompassed not only Jewish butchers and money changers but millers, grain merchants, and jewelers as well. In later volumes Jews appear as physicians, blacksmiths, cloth merchants, spice dealers, pearl stringers, tailors, carpenters, soap dealers and soap manufacturers, cobblers, tax collectors, and more.[11]

This variegated activity sheds new light on the dynamic side of the economic scene. It also offers us profound and unexpected insights into the more static side of Jewish existence. Although the stereotypical picture of Jews as unproductive, parasitic beggars living on charity collected in the Diaspora and sent to the Holy Land to support them is partially maintained in scattered references in the registers, totally new dimensions emerge from the plethora of

---

[10] *Encyclopaedia of Islam*, new edition (henceforth cited as *EI*^{2}), s.v. "Akhī Bābā."
[11] *Jewish Life*, pp. 140-198; *Economic Life*, pp. 29, 101.

information provided by this source. The central authorities were led to believe that all Jews in Jerusalem should pay the lowest poll tax rates because of their poverty; they could not have been completely misinformed. But the closer look at daily life that the *sijill* affords us, reveals that at least some of the Jews were quite well-off. The availability of significant sums of money was a *sine qua non* for the proper functioning of the Jewish moneylenders and money changers referred to above. This was also true for jewelers, as well as for merchants involved in international trade in the Ottoman Empire and around the Mediterranean basin. The few legacies of Jews included in our documents are not definitive: Jews probably tried to hide as many of their belongings as possible from the local authorities in order to avoid taxation. Indications of the contents of some Jewish households may, however, be gleaned from inheritance renferences found in the *sijill*. The most reliable sources for this are, once again, not explicit reports, but rather transactions involving real estate recorded either posthumously or concurrently with the actual sale or purchase. These show beyond any doubt that Jews, both men and women, owned tracts of land, apartments, and buildings of a private and public nature. Some are described in a general manner, noting that their location was a matter of common knowledge, while others are provided with detailed descriptions, both of the property itself and of the plots adjoining its four sides. This valuable information may enable future scholars to reconstruct the map of Jewish households in Ottoman Jerusalem. At this stage it adds a new dimension to our understanding of the very nature of Jewish life there: more than one hundred different units of real estate have been identified beyond any reasonable doubt as belonging to different Jewish owners during the 16th century. Many others were designated as rented by Jews for a long period of time. All these new elements combined will drastically change the prevailing conventional wisdom: in Ottoman Jerusalem, alongside Jewish paupers there were others who led a reasonably prosperous life, or at least could afford one. The Jewish lady who imported special Italian marble for the renovation of her bathroom may have been exceptionally extravagant, but she was nonetheless a member of the Jewish community. So were other Jewish women who permanently employed maids in their homes or owned impressive quantities of jewels.

The Muslim religious court served as the main stage on which all these stories were told and where all these proceedings were recorded. Jewish presence there, as problematic as this may seem from a traditional halakhic perspective, was of no particular meaning as far as this stronghold of traditional Islam was concerned. No special allowances were made to accommodate the Jews. For example, they were summoned to the court, and appeared, on any day of the week, including the Sabbath.[12] Jewish women appeared in court, were publicly identified and then openly testified on all matters, including some of a highly personal nature. The Jews went to the Muslim court for a variety of reasons, but the overwhelming fact was their ongoing and almost permanent presence there. This indicates that they went there not only in search of justice, but did so hoping, or rather knowing, that more often than not they would attain

---

[12] See, for example, 76/226 (d-e), and also 36/68 below.

redress when wronged. The social and administrative role of the Ottoman kadi in Jerusalem and elsewhere still awaits proper research and analysis. But even in the relatively narrow and limited context of his relationship with the Jews, one may conclude from the information of the *sijill* that he played a very important role in reporting their grievances to the central authorities. He also protected the Jews against recurring attempts of harassment by ever-changing cadres of local dignitaries and civil-servants.

We shall return later to an evaluation of the harassment to which Jews were subjected. At this point some elaboration on their very presence in the Muslim court is called for. The Jews went to court to resolve much more than their conflicts with Muslim or Christian neighbors. They turned to the *sharī'a* authorities to seek redress with respect to internal differences, and even in matters within their immediate family (intimate relations between husband and wife, *nafaqa* maintenance payments to divorcees, support of infants etc.). Quite often and as a matter of course they presented documents in Hebrew for consultation, confirmation, or translation when necessary. The Hebrew language was not only present in documents, it was also heard spoken by litigants whose depositions or testimonies a Jewish interpreter would translate for the court. Sometimes the original Hebrew form was even recorded without the Muslim scribe realizing that he was actually writing Hebrew words in Arabic script. Along with Hebrew names and terms, other matters of a purely Jewish religious nature were introduced into the Muslim court: Jewish prayer shawls and phylacteries, Jewish traditional and communal institutions, Jewish holidays and even Jewish dreams (the latter in conjunction with attempts of certain Jews to enter, or at least get as close as possible to, the Temple Mount, from which they were absolutely banned). And notwithstanding the omnipresence and exclusivity of Islam in this institution, oath-taking on the Torah was a matter of routine when Jewish endowments were established, inheritance lists were read out, or cases involving Jewish testimony (in conjunction with members of the military or civilian establishment as well as with reference to other members of their own community) were adjudicated.

These references add up to the Muslim court's acceptance of things Jewish and should be seen as stemming from the basic concept of Jews as being part a larger group, that of *ahl al-kitāb*, "the people of the book," and therefore an integral part of the system, although different. They should also be viewed in relation to the other term used in conjunction with the Jews, i.e. *ahl al-dhimma*, "the protected people," those who deserve and enjoy the full protection of the state. Their possessions were protected, although they might have had to pay for extra protection at night for their houses and commercial properties. Their title deeds and other official documents indicating their rights were honored when presented to the court, being treated like those of their Muslim neighbors. A missing person, whether Muslim or Jewish, would be searched for and if a corpse was found it would have to be reported to the authorities, explained, and minutely examined. Nevertheless, the concept of particularity underlay all their activities and their very presence within the Muslim society. Attempts of the Jews to run their communal affairs independently, without involvement of any state apparatus, were systematically upheld by the central and provincial authorities, except for occasional interference for purposes of verifying facts as reported by their representatives. The latter were not only the officially nominated "heads" of the community, but also their judges (*dayyān*), their slaughterers, ushers and cantors in their synagogues, and caretakers of their equally autonomously run cemeteries. Although the term *millet,* used to denote their particular administrative organization, would be introduced in this special meaning only years later, the general form and particular substance implied by this term in the years of Ottoman decline during the 19th century existed in practice as early as the regime's 16th-century heyday.[13]

In reference to the organization of Jewish communal life, one more qualification should be added. Although, following the *sijill,* we have been referring to the Jews as a single community distinguished from the other demographic elements, we should bear in mind that there also were certain subcategories applied at that time. "Jews," without any qualifying adjective, refers to "Sephardic Jews," or even the wider category of Oriental Jews. These constituted the majority of the community, and were distinguished from the Ashkenazic Jews, referred to as *alaman*, "German." Less frequently a reference is made to *musta'riba* Jews ("those who assumed the looks and behavior of the local Arabs") or *'ifranj* Jews ("Frankish," European–a term that also denoted Roman Catholics). There was also the differentiation between Karaite and Rabbanite Jews. These various qualifying adjectives indicate that there were perceptible differences.

---

[13] See "On the Realities of the *Millet* System: Jerusalem in the Sixteenth Century" in *Christians and Jews in the Ottoman Empire*, ed. B. Braude and B. Lewis (New York, 1982), 2:7-18.

But it was the Jews themselves who drew the differentiating lines and the *sijill* only reflected the terms they brought before the judge. The authorities showed little interest in these various categories; they regarded the "Jewish community" as one whole, differentiated only occasionally and upon specific request.

Finally, an evaluation and appraisal of the situation of the Jews in Ottoman Jerusalem would be incomplete without an attempt to answer the basic question: Did they go about their business happily or were they oppressed? Should the bottom line of the "balance sheet" be written in red or blue? Was the picture black or white? There is no simple answer to these questions. As an illustration let us look at the inheritance laws. Jews of course preferred to apply their own laws, both as part of the principled endeavor to apply the halakhah and as a result of practical considerations, such as avoiding, for example, the confiscation by the Muslim authorities of unclaimed assets of an heirless deceased person, as was the norm with respect to unclaimed possessions. The picture emerging from the *sijill* documents is somewhat baffling. On the one hand we encounter recurring Sultanic decrees sent to Jerusalem–in response to pleas of the Jews–to the effect that "nothing should be done to stop them from applying their own laws" regarding a variety of matters. There are also many explicit references to the overriding importance of applying *sharī‘a* laws to them only if they so choose. On the other hand, if we look closely at some of the inheritance lists, we see that the local court allocated to female members of Jewish families half the share given to male members, exactly as in Islamic law. This meant, *ipso facto*, a significant improvement in the status of Jewish women with respect to legacies over that accorded them by Jewish tradition, although it actually meant the application of Islamic law in an internal Jewish context.

There are signs of discriminatory policies applied both implicitly and explicitly to the Jews. When a Muslim takes an oath in court and concludes it with a solemn undertaking that if he fails to uphold it "may I become Jewish," clear light is shed on the conception of the local population as to the actual meaning of being a Jew in their midst. This is further accentuated by the custom of the operator of the local bathhouse who provided clean towels to Muslim urban customers, and dirty or torn ones to the villagers–and to the Jews. The bathhouse gives us further insights into the naked truth. After entering it, Jews could not be distinguished from others since all removed their clothing, which included the identifying yellow "patch" Jews had to wear. To avoid unnecessary embarrassment to the Muslim customers who used the same facility, the Jews were required to wear a small bell to announce their arrival so that the Muslims could cover themselves with their towels. The 'Umar covenant (e.g. policies prohibiting the erection of new places of worship, regulations limiting the height of Jewish buildings, etc.) as well as other discriminatory regulations were consistently applied. Finally, there were specific cases of conversion to Islam of male and female members of the Jewish community.

All of this corresponds to what were considered entrenched patterns of Muslim discrimination against Jews. But as we have shown, the picture emerging from the *sijill* documents adds many new elements and gives their reality totally different dimensions.

Oppressive and arbitrary policies of provincial rulers toward their subjects were very common, a norm that was applied to Jews, Christians and Muslims alike. The religious establishment might also have been expected to ill-treat the Jews, but the kadi routinely acted otherwise: he defended Jewish causes jeopardized by high-handed behavior of local governors; he enabled Jewish business people and craftsmen to lease properties from Muslim endowments on an equal footing with Muslim bidders; more generally, he respected their rituals and places of worship and guarded them against encroachment even when the perpetrators were other Muslim dignitaries.

The most telling information gleaned from these archives are the positive insights the court cases afford, not through the judicial perspective which of course is of primary significance, but rather through secondary or even tertiary perspectives. We become aware of the wide range of professional activities of the Jews which included almost all occupations; we learn of the relative prosperity of at least part of the community, as indicated by Jewish ownership of property and by their spending habits, unrestricted travel, business contacts, and activities throughout the Ottoman Empire and beyond. True, their inferior status was built into the system, but in practical terms it affected their daily life or patterns of behavior in a relatively limited way. No wonder, therefore, that the number of Jews living in Jerusalem increased significantly over the years, consonant with the changes in the Muslim population. They may not have been perfectly happy with some of the limitations to which they were subjected but they learned to live with or to circumvent many of them. No one interfered with their internal organization or their external cultural and economic activities. They seem to have internalized their social inferiority without much apparent hostility. In a world where civil and political equality, or positive social change affecting the group or even the individual were not the norms, the Sultan's Jewish subjects had no reason to mourn their status or begrudge their conditions of life. The Jews of Ottoman Jerusalem enjoyed religious and administrative autonomy within an Islamic state, and as a constructive, dynamic element of the local economy and society they could–and actually did–contribute to its functioning. The 16th century should, therefore, be viewed as a formative period with respect to the Jewish presence in Ottoman Jerusalem. Beyond that time the context underwent certain changes that affected the condition of the Jews, but the basic patterns moulded as early as the 16th century remained for generations to come.

Volume 1
(1530 - 1531)

10 (a) Dhū'l-Qa'da, 936: A soap factory[14] was constructed in the Jewish quarter (*ḥārat al-yahūd*)[15] as part of the endowment (*waqf*) of b. Abū-Sharīf.

11 A detailed description (costs, technical data, wages) of constructing the aforementioned soap factory.

15 (c) Middle of Dhū'l-Qa'da, 936: A Jewish slaughterer (*dhabbāḥ*)[16] may slaughter only Mondays, Thursdays, & holidays in the slaughterhouse (*maslakh ḥārat al-yahūd)* of the Jewish quarter.

22 (c) 20 Dhū'l-Qa'da, 936: The head of the Jewish community (*shaykh al-yahūd*) may not purchase any silver from the jewelers' market (*sūq al-ṣāgha*).[17]

131 (a) 20 Rabī' al-Awwal, 937: A Jew arrested for a monetary debt to a Muslim.

131 (f) 22 Rabī' al-Awwal, 937: A Jew underwrites (*kafāla*)[18] another Jew in court.

197 (d) 29 Jumādā'l-Awwal, 937: A Jewish jeweler undertakes to refrain from public drinking of wine, troublemaking, or cursing of the community leaders (*dayyān, rayyis, shaykh*).

218 (d) 17 Jumādā'l-Ākhir, 937: The body of a Jewish grain merchant (*ḥaddār*) was found outside the Jewish quarter. Both his married daughter and his wife testified that he had spent time buying grain in the

[14] On soap factories, see *Economic Life*, pp. 61-74.
[15] On *ḥārat al-yahūd*, see *Jewish Life*, pp. 206-209.
[16] On the ritual slaughterer, see ibid., pp. 155-159.
[17] On *shaykh al-yahūd*, see ibid., pp. 36-58. On the jewelers' guild and its activities, see "Gold and Silver Crafting in Ottoman Jerusalem."
[18] *EI*^{2}. s.v."kafāla."

district of Banī Zayd. When he had reached the village of Dayr Ghassāna he died of a natural cause.

225 (b) 16 Sha'bān, 937: A Jew converted to Islam[19] while on a boat from Egypt to Tripoli, and then was seen in Jerusalem wearing Jewish clothes, including the yellow headgear.

369 (c) 23 Dhū'l-Ḥijja, 937: A janissary sold half of the equipment of a mill to a Karaite Jew, who paid less than half the amount pledged.

370 (b) 23 Dhū'l-Ḥijja, 938: A Muslim owes the above Jew 1,000 *ḥalabiyya*[20] silver coins (the exact amount of the aforementioned outstanding debt).

380 (c) 6 Muḥarram, 938: The *yasaqjī* appointed Shmū'īl the Karaite–in accordance with an order that arrived from the Pasha in Damascus–to be a money changer (*ṣayrafī*) in Jerusalem and to differentiate between real and counterfeit coins.

383 (a) 7 Muḥarram, 938: Yahūdā b. Mūsā, the money changer of the two Exalted endowments (i.e. those of the Temple Mount in Jerusalem and the Tombs of the Patriarchs in Hebron) owes 9,000 *dirham* to a Muslim as the last installment on a debt exceeding 36,000.

420 (a) 15 Ṣafar, 938: A Muslim from the village of Jīb al-Fukhkhār accused Yahūdā b. Ibrāhīm of owing his mother 10 silver *funduqī* and 4 silver *zōlta*(?) that she had deposited with him.

---

[19] On the conversion of Jews to Islam, see *Jewish Life*, pp. 74-76.

[20] On *qiṭ'a ḥalabiyya*, see *Economic Life*, pp. 48-53.

Volume 2
(1538)

70 (a-b) 10 Sha‘bān, 938: A very long and detailed list of jewelry that had been missing from the house of Sulaymān the Jew and belonged to Dhahabā, the Jewish beautician (*kaḥḥāla*). A Muslim who was brought to the court by the head of the night watchers admitted to have stolen them from her room two days earlier and buried them in a dung-heap in a mill that belonged to a Muslim. The Jewish woman was asked to report those pieces that she was missing.

92 (d) 10 Ramaḍān, 938: For 40 years the Ashkenazi (*faranjī*)[21] rabbi (*dayyān*), Ya‘qūb b. Yahūdā, leased a plot of land bordering on the Jewish cemetery from the two kadis entitled to lease it.

112 (b) 7 Shawwāl, 938: Dā’ūd b. Shmū’īl Shūshān in his capacity as the testator (*waṣiyy*) of the Jewish child Ibrahīm b. Isḥāq Shulāl, received from the Karaite Ṣadaqa b. Yūsif the debt he owed the child's deceased father according to a Hebrew language document. The sum paid was at the Istanbul exchange rate for the sum of 100,000 *‘uthmānī* silver coins.

126 (a) 23 Shawwāl, 938: Three Jews–"master" (*mu‘allim*) Mūsā b. Ḥayyim, Malk ī b. Yahūdā, and Yūsif b. Mūsā–leased from the Muslim authorities a plot of land "for the burial of their dead." It was part of the Jismāniyya endowment and was leased for a period of thirty years as of 940 for the sum of 2,250 *qiṭ‘a sulaymāniyya* silver coins.[22]

137-138 3 Dhū'l-Qa‘da, 938: Yūsif the Jewish money changer (*ṣayrafī*) of the governor of Jerusalem and Gaza collected from a long list of Muslim, Jewish, and Christian merchants substantial amounts of money for

[21] *EI*², s.v. "Ifrandj."

[22] On Jewish cemeteries in Jerusalem, see *Jewish Life*, pp. 86-101.

which the governor promised to provide them with olive oil. The largest sums were paid by the Christian, and even more by the Jewish communities in lump sums.

144 (c) 15 Dhū'l-Qa'da, 938: A Muslim from the village of Māliḥa sold Sa'īd b. Mūsā b. Tamām the Rabbanite Jewish spice dealer one quarter of an orchard located in the village of Bayt Mazmīl for the sum of 300 *'uthmānī*[23] silver coins.

144 (d) 15 Dhū'l-Qa'da, 938: The head builder of Jerusalem undertook to build for the Karaite Jew "master" Ṣadaqa the money changer, parts of his house in the Karaite Jewish neighborhood (*ḥāra*) for the sum of 2,000 *'uthmānī* silver coins.

210 (b) 27 Muḥarram, 939: The Jewess Ḥannā b. Hārūn declared that after her death the house she owned in the Jewish neighborhood (*ḥāra)* will become part of the endowment for the poor of the community.

---

[23] See "Note on Weights, Measures and Monetary Values" in *Economic Life*, pp. 129-130.

Volume 3
(1533)

149 (b) A copy of the *jizya*[24] tax register of the Jews and Christians in Jerusalem, brought by 'Alī *chā'ūsh*[25] for the year 940: 30 Jewish names, rates, payments (*siyāqat* script).

273 (b) 14 Rabī' al-Awwal, 940: 22 Jews from Jerusalem (names given) owe Fatḥ al-Dīn the silversmith (*ṣā'igh*) 16,000 (?) *ḥalabiyya* (*siyāqat*) they had borrowed from him. Two other Jews personally underwrite (*kafāla*) this debt.

324 (e) 23 Rabī' al-Ākhir, 940: A Maltese Jew is brought by the inspector of the markets (*muḥtasib*)[26] who found his weight stones to be defective.

324 (f) 23 Rabī' al-Ākhir, 940: A Jewish spice dealer (*'aṭṭār*) admitted that he had sold soap at a rate 20 percent higher than the one officially announced.

---

[24] *EI*², s.v. "Djizya"; *Jewish Life*, pp. 20-27.

[25] A member of the Corps of Pursuivants, often sent on behalf of the central authorities on official duty to the provinces. See also U. Heyd, *Ottoman Documents on Palestine, 1552-1615* (London, 1960), p. 54, n. 5.

[26] On the office of *ḥisba*, see *Economic Life*, pp. 11-16.

Volume 4
(1534 - 1535)

15 (c) 13 Sha'bān, 940: A Jew Shiāda b. Shamīla bought 2 *qinṭārs* of rice from another Jew, Nasīm b. Mūsā b. 'Ammāsh, for the amount of 1,950 *ḥalabiyya*. This sum was subtracted from an outstanding debt between the two.

36 (c) 27 Sha'bān, 940: The Jew Nasīm b. Mūsā b. 'Ammāsh owes Sīdī 'Alā al-Dīn 2,100 *ḥalabiyya* for 2 *qinṭārs* of rice he bought from him. 'Azīzā b. Nāṣir, Nas īm's mother, and another Jew put up security for this debt, and the former even mortgaged a two floor building she owned (near al-Maslakh soap factory) to ensure payment of the debt.

43 (f) 3 Ramaḍān, 940: The two heads (*ra'īs*) of the Jewish community, Mūsā b. Ḥayyim and Faraj-Allah b. Makhlūf, undertake to pay 1,000 *'uthmānī* to the Dome of the Rock if they fail to report deaths in their community.

109 (b) 18 Shawwāl, 940: Mūsā b. Ḥayyim and Faraj-Allah al-Jawjarī undertook to pay a penalty (*jarīma*) of 1,000 *'uthmānī* if they failed to report any death–male or female–of Jews, whether they left heirs or any belongings that had to be reported to the "treasury" of heirless legacies (*bayt al-māl*), [and transferred thereto].

109 (e) 18 Shawwāl, 940: The Jewess Qamar b. Salamūn *al-faranjiyya* testified in front of Tāj al-Dīn al-Sukkarī, in charge of the "treasury" of heirless legacies (*bayt al-māl*),[27] as to the few clothes she owned, being one of the Jewish beggars.

114 (b) 24 Shawwāl, 940: Shū'ā, a Jewish tanner (*adamī*, one who separates the fat from the hide) was found dead. Other tanners testified that they were practicing their

---

[27] On *bayt al-māl*, see A. Cohen and B. Lewis, *Population and Revenue in the Towns of Palestine in the Sixteenth Century* (Princeton, 1978), pp. 73-75, n. 90.

profession with him in the countryside, and when they reached the village of Bayt al-Mā' he contracted the plague (*ṭā'ūn*) and died.

128 (b) 3 Dhū'l-Qa'da, 940: Tāj al-Dīn al-Sukkarī accused the Jew Minäḥim al-Zalabānī of importing (*jalab*) various commodities from the hinterland (*al-barr*) including cheese, which he sells to the Muslims at exorbitant prices. He confessed.

188 (c) 16 Dhū'l-Ḥijja, 940: Ya'qūb b. Isḥāq the Rabbanite (*rabbān*) Jew authorized Līwī b. Ya'qūb, the Jewish *dayyān* to collect and temporarily keep whatever belonged to his wife in case she died while he was traveling out of town.

198 (a) 21 Dhū'l-Ḥijja, 940: A Hebronite claimed that Mūsā b. Yaḥyā the Jewish tanner (*adamī*) owes him 2,600 *ḥalabiyya* for water buffalo (*jāmūs*) hides. He acknowledged the debt, but claimed he had paid it all except for 130 *ḥalabiyya*.

277 (a) 8 Ṣafar, 941: The wife of Shamīla b. Ya'qūb the Jew established an endowment (*waqf*): an orchard (*ghirās*) of fig and apple trees, vines etc. she inherited from her father and owned in the Bayt Iksā village.

305 (d) 13 Ṣafar, 941: Mūsā b. Minäḥīm, head and spokesman (*mutakallim*) for the Jewish community, guaranteed that no Jews will weigh any wheat outside "the vacant lot of the grains" (*'arṣat al-ghilāl*)[28] in the presence of its operators.

305 (f) 13 Ṣafar, 941: A Muslim contests the rights of Mūsā b. Minäḥīm the Jew to a vegetable garden (*ḥākūra*) adjacent to the latter's house in the al-Rīsha quarter. Upon inspection the court confirmed that the vegetable garden belonged to the Jew.

365 (c) 25 Rabī' al-Awwal, 941: A Muslim buys from the Jew Mūsā b. 'Abd al-'Āl (?) who was the expert (*mu'allim*) in the mint (*dār al-ḍarb*) of Damascus half an olive

---

[28] See *Economic Life*, pp. 106-112.

grove the Jew had bought in 927 in the village of Ṣūr Bāhir.

410 (a) 24 Rabīʿ al-Ākhir, 941: End of a testimony of Jewish witnesses as to the inheritance of a deceased Jew.

410 (d) 24 Rabīʿ al-Ākhir, 941: Nūnā b. Rūbīn the Jewess accused Nasīm b. Mūsā of having called her a prostitute. She brought two witnesses and upon confirmation of her complaint the defendant was flogged (*taʿzīr*).[29]

417 (a) 27 Rabīʿ al-Ākhir, 941: Tāj al-Dīn, the inspector of the markets (*muḥtasib*) in charge of the "treasury" of *bayt al-māl* declared that he received a sum of money in gold coins (*sikka*) from Mūsā b. Ḥayyim, the head of the Jewish community, probably 16 (blurred *siyāqat*) that another Jew had deposited with him.

526 (c) 28 Jumādā'l-Ākhir, 941: Mūsā b. Ḥayyim, Faraj-Allah al-Jawjarī, Malkī b. Yahūdā, Minaḥim–heads of the Jewish community–claimed that according to a Sultanic order before his death, they had paid the Shāfiʿī kadi the poll tax (*jizya*) they owed for the year 941 in the amount of 5,400 *ʿuthmānī* (15 per day). They also presented receipts (*rajʿa*) to this effect.

555 (d) 13 Rajab, 941: The Jews Ḥayyim b. Ibrāhīm and Faraj-Allah b. Ḥayyim, testify in support of a janissary's claim that a Christian had hit him with a stone.

612 (a) 1 Ramaḍān, 941: New copper coins (*fulūs*) were brought from Damascus to be introduced in exchange for silver. The Jewish money changers' quota is 2,900 *ʿuthmānī* and it was given to Mūsā b. Ḥayyim and Faraj-Allah al-Jawjarī (The quota for Muslims is 4,000 *ʿuthmānī*, for Christians 2,000).

612 (c) 18 Ramaḍān, 941: The above messenger confirmed the receipt of 2,900 *ʿuthmānī* from the Jewish community as per the above transaction.

---

[29] *Encyclopaedia of Islam* (henceforth cited as *EI*), s.v. "Taʿzīr"; E. Tyan, *Histoire de l'organisation judiciaire en pays d'Islam* (Leiden, 1960), pp. 569-570; U. Heyd, *Studies in Old Ottoman Criminal Law* (Oxford, 1973), pp. 271-275.

Volume 5
(1535 - 1536)

7 (b) 1 Dhū'l-Qa'da, 941: Sulaymān b. Ya'qūb the Jew and his companions owe the officer in charge of law and order (*ṣūbāshī*) of Hebron 6 arm lengths (*dhirā'*)[30] of *jawkh* cloth for escorting them in their pilgrimage (*ziyāra*) from Jerusalem to Hebron and back, as well as another 5 *dhirā'* for the road tax (*khafar*)[31] he paid for them.

9 (g) 3 Dhū'l-Qa'da, 941: A North African Jewish woman pledged that she would never sell *laban* yogurt to Jews unless it is good quality, for the price of 2 silver *dirhams*[32] per *raṭl*.

50 (d) 5 Dhū'l-Ḥijja, 941: Yahūdā, the Jewish money changer paid the preacher (*khaṭīb*) of the al-Aqṣā Mosque 520 *'uthmānī* on account of the *jizya* for the year 941.

82 (a) 18 Dhū'l-Ḥijja, 941: Manṣūr b. 'Abd Allāh, the Damascene Jew living in Jerusalem, endowed (*waqf*) his share (25 percent) of an orchard (*ghirās*, fig and apple trees, vines, etc.). The other partners in this orchard are also Jewish.

82 (c) 18 Dhū'l-Ḥijja, 941: A Muslim sold Mināḥim b. Qaṭān the Jew 25 percent of an orchard in the al-Sharaf quarter for 4,750 *ḥalabiyya*.

94 (e) 5 Muḥarram, 942: Mūsā b. Yahūdā the Jew established an endowment (*waqf*) of his share (25 percent) of an orchard (fig trees, vines etc.) in the village of Bayt Ṣafāfā. The beneficiary was the Dome of the Rock.

---

[30] *EI*², s.v. "Dhirā'."

[31] See Cohen and Lewis, *Population and Revenue*, pp. 56-58, 72.

[32] See *Economic Life*, pp. 48-53; *EI*², s.v. "Dirham"; W. Hinz, *Islamische Masse und Gewichte* (Leiden, 1970), pp. 1-8.

98 (c) 7 Muḥarram, 942: Ghāliya b. Sa'dūn Qallāsh who was the wife of Isḥāq the Jew, established an endowment of an orchard she owned in the village of Bayt Ṣafāfā, as well as 50 percent of another orchard located in the subdistrict (*nāḥiya*) that she owned in partnership with a Muslim from the village of al-Māliḥa.

115 (b) 14 Muḥarram, 942: The Jewish *dayyān*, Lāwī b. Ya'qūb, approached the Ḥanafī kadi. Yūsuf b. Sa'īd *al-ḥāmī*, already married, wants to marry 'Azīzā b. Shiḥāta the daughter of his sister; would such a marriage be valid? The kadi quoted Abū Ḥanīfa on similar issues and gave an affirmative ruling.

125 (d) 20 Muḥarram, 942: The operators of "the vacant lot of the grains" agreed with Mūsā, the head of the Jewish community (*shaykh ṭā'ifat al-yahūd*) that the Jewish grain merchants (*ḥaddār*) will not be liable for *ghafar* road tax on the wheat they bring into town.

156 (e) 8 Ṣafar, 942: The Jewess Astīr b. Mūsā testified that her husband, Yūsuf b. Sulaymān, also present in court, as well as her brother Mūsā, will inherit all her belongings (list provided).

208 (b) 18 Rabī' al-Awwal, 942: Khalīfa the Jew recited the two *shahādas* and declared that he converted to Islam.

249 (c) 13 Rabī' al-Ākhir, 942: Mināḥīm b. Hāyin is accused of unlawful possession of half of a house in the al-Rīsha quarter. He claimed to have been given it as a pledge by the head of the blacksmiths guild.

249 (d) 12 Rabī' al-Ākhir, 942: Isḥāq b. 'Anāh (?) and Shlūmū al-Bārūd, both Jewish, undertook to sell meat in the Jewish quarter to the Jewish community.

337 (e) 14 Jumādā'l-Ākhir, 942: The expert (*al-mu'allim*) butcher, Aḥmad b. al-Duhayna, pledged not to sell any meat to Jews during this month.

366 (b) 8 Rajab, 942: A woman's corpse was found in the Jewish quarter (*ḥārat al-yahūd*) the Jewish community buried her without the mandatory permit of the person in charge of *bayt al-māl*.

Volume 6
(1536 - 1537)

36 (b) 24 Muḥarram, 943: A Muslim woman from Gaza claimed that Shlūmū b. Hārūn the Moroccan (*al-maghribī*), a Jewish spice dealer in the same town, owed her 10,000 *ḥalabiyya* invested as a limited partnership (*muḍāraba*). The defendant conceded only 3,000, adding that she had at her disposal a written pledge in Hebrew script given to her by his son, now living in Gaza.

38 (c) 25 Muḥarram, 943: A Hebronite testified that he had received from the Jew Sulaymān b. Mūsā 4 *raṭls* of indigo to be delivered to a customer in Safed. If any part of the consignment is lost, he pledged to pay 3 *ashrafī* gold coins (i.e. 150 *dirham ḥalabiyya*) per *raṭl*.

47 (d) 29 Muḥarram, 943: A complaint was made in court by a group of Muslims, Christians, and Jews against official functionaries who allegedly extorted money from them.

55 (c) 4 Ṣafar, 943: Ḥabīb b. Ibrāhīm and Sāsūn b. Yaḥyā, Jewish blacksmiths (*ḥaddād*), pledged that they would not practice their profession outside Jerusalem without the knowledge of the head of their guild. If any of them does not abide by this rule he will pay a 1,000 *'uthmānī* penalty to the *ṣūbāshī*.

299 (c) 18 Rajab, 943: Mūsā b. Isḥāq, a Jewish cobbler, declared that he was "a beggar from among the Jewish beggars" and that his few belongings will be inherited by his nephew, Mūsā.

346 (c) 2 Ramaḍān, 943: A cavalry officer (*sipāhī*)[33] received from the Jew Shū'ā b. 'Āzir *al-maghribī* 160 (*siyāqat*) *qiṭ'a sulaymāniyya* collected from the village of Bayt

[33] *EI*, s.v. "Sepoy."

Ṭilmā which is part of the former's "feudal" fief (*tīmār*).[34]

408 (a) 13 Shawwāl, 943: Aṣlān b. Fraym the Jew guaranteed the outstanding debt of Yūsif b. Mūsā the Jew as part of an earlier purchase of cloth.

424 (a) 8 Dhū'l-Qa'da, 943: Tāj al-Dīn al-Sukkarī testified (with the confirmation of two silversmiths) that all that accrues to the Sultan through the silversmiths' (*ṣāgha*) guild from the pilgrims during the "season" (*mawsim*) is traditionally divided between the Jewish and Christian guild members at the rate of one-third and two-thirds, respectively.

436 (c) 16 Shawwāl, 944: Three Muslim brothers sell to the Jew Ibrāhīm b. Yūsif, known as Kāshtrū through his authorized agent (*wakīl*), *al-mu'allim* Yūsif b. Sulaymān, all the ruins of a castle (*qaṣr*) previously built outside Jerusalem in Arḍ Manjik for 2,000 (?) *'uthmānī* (end of document missing).

489 (c) 18 Dhū'l-Ḥijja, 943: A Muslim sold a mare to Shū'ā b. 'Āzir the Moroccan (*maghribī*) Jew for 600 *ḥalabiyya.*

489 (d) 18 Dhū'l-Ḥijja, 943: A Muslim leased a mill (*ṭāḥūn*) in the Jewish quarter to Sulaymān b. Ya'qūb the Egyptian Jew, and to the above-mentioned Shū'ā b. 'Āzir for the year 944.

489 (e) The above-mentioned Sulaymān bought a mare from a timariot, then discovered that it had a defect, so he requested the court to cancel the deal (end of document missing).

497 (a) 23 Dhū'l-Ḥijja, 943: The Rabbanite Jewess Dūnā b. Ya'qūb, Ibrahīm 'Amrān's wife, rented a house in the Jewish quarter from a Mālikī kadi for 4 years. The entire rent was 2,600 *ḥalabiyya*, half of which she will spend on repairs.

506 (a) 1 Muḥarram, 944: The Muslim comptroller (*nāẓir*) of the Ṭawāshī endowment leased a bakery (*furn*) in the

---

[34] *EI*, s.v. "Tīmār."

Jewish quarter to ‘Allūsh the Jew for a one year period and for the sum of 14 *‘uthmānī* to be paid at the end of each month.

591 (a) 28 Ṣafar, 944: Sulaymān b. Ya‘qūb b. Dā’ūd and Sha‘shū‘ b. ‘Ayzar, both Rabbanite Jews, testified that they were partners of a Muslim in operating a mill known as *ṭāḥūn b. nā’ib al-qal‘a* in the Jewish quarter. Among the details of each partner's duties, Sulaymān will provide the grains and Shā‘shū‘ will do the actual grinding.

661 (b) 7 Rabī‘ al-Ākhir, 944: The Rabbanite Jew Shmū’īl b. Ibrāhīm testified as to the details of his belongings: some clothing, one-third of a house in the Jewish quarter in Cairo. He had sold his shop in Cairo to his grandson for 1,500 *dirham ḥalabiyya*, and as for his belongings in his shop in the spice dealers' market in Jerusalem, they should be sold upon his death, the money should be spent on his burial, and the balance should go to his daughter.

712 (b) 4 Jumādā'l-Awwal, 944: Upon inspection the one-half *'ūqiyya* weight of Mūsā the Jew was found somewhat faulty.

712 (c) 4 Jumādā'l-Awwal, 944: Upon inspection the one *'ūqiyya* weight of ‘Alī Jūkār the Jew was found very faulty.

712 (d) 4 Jumādā'l-Awwal, 944: The one *'ūqiyya* weight of the Maltese Jew was found very faulty upon inspection and his one-half *raṭl* weight was found lacking 15 *dirham*s.

715 (b) 16 Jumādā'l-’Ūlā, 944: The Jewish tax collectors (*‘āmil*s)[35] in Gaza, Sulaymān and Shamīl, sent the sum of 9,706 *qiṭ‘a*, collected as road tax (*khafar*), for the construction of the walls of Jerusalem in the name of the governor of Gaza.[36]

715 (d) 16 Jumādā'l-’Ūlā, 944: The above-mentioned transferred for the same purpose via a janissary soldier

---

[35] *EI*^{2}, s.v. "‘Āmil."

[36] See "The Walls of Jerusalem," cited above.

4,250 *qiṭ'a* out of the taxes collected in the *khāṣṣ*[37] dominions in Gaza.

715 (e) [No Date mentioned.] The above-mentioned Sulaymān and Shamīl transferred for the same purpose another installment of 10,782 *qiṭ'a* as road tax in Gaza.

---

[37] For this and related terms, see *Population and Revenue*, pp.41-43.

Volume 7
(1537 - 1538)

9 (b) 8 Jumādā'l-Awwal, 944: A Muslim sold *al-mu'allim* Yahūdā the Jewish silversmith a consignment of sesame for the sum of 2,000 *'uthmānī.*

19 (a) 14 Jumādā'l-Awwal, 944: *Al-mu'allim* Aliās b. Mūsā, the Jewish tailor, claimed that the heirs of a deceased soldier from the Jerusalem Citadel owe him 38 *ḥalabiyya* for a piece of cloth he had sold their father as well as for his work sewing it.

21 (a) 15 Jumādā'l-'Ūlā, 944: 'Alī b. Za'rūr and Falāq b. Ya'qūb b. Ḥayyim, both Jewish, testified to having received from the *ṣūbāshī* of Jerusalem the sum of 500 *'uthmānī* that had been unlawfully levied from their community. An order to this effect was sent by the governor of Jerusalem and Gaza when he discovered that two sums of 500 each were levied from the Jewish and Christian communities.

131 (c-d) 27 Jumādā'l-Ākhir, 944: The body of a Jewish boy, Dānī b. Ma'tūq, was discovered in a dilapidated building, with signs indicating murder. The *ṣūbāshī* inspected the site, near the *zāwiya* of *Shaykh* al-Balāsī.

166 (b) 9 Rajab, 944: *Al-mu'allim* 'Abd al-Laṭīf b. Ṣadaqa b. Yūsif, whose father was the Jewish money changer in the mint of Damascus, acknowledged the debt of 5,400 *'uthmānī* to the Shāfi'ī kadi: half of it for a loan for 9 months, extended in gold coins. The Jewish physician 'Abd al-Karīm b. Mūsā and the Jew Ibrāhīm b. Shmu'īl guaranteed the entire debt for him.

360 (a) 18 Ramaḍān, 944: Three Muslim brothers confirmed that in the year 912 their deceased mother had sold her house in the Ḥayādira quarter to 'Āzir b. Ibrahīm, alias Zaradīn the Jew.

374 (f) 25 Ramaḍān, 944: Ya'qūb, the head (*shaykh*) of the Jewish community in Jerusalem was arrested on the charge of nonpayment of the tithe (*'ushr*) tax owed for the lease of the Jewish cemetery from the al-Ṣalāḥiyya endowment.

394 (c) 5 Shawwāl, 944: The Rabbanite Jew *al-mu'allim* Mūsā b. Da'ūd, alias b. *al-sabīl* divorced his wife, Rāḥīl b. Ya'qūb the Cairene Jewess, in the Muslim court.

411 (a) 10 Shawwāl, 944: *Al-mu'allim* Yūsif b. Sulaymān the Jew was authorized by Ibrāhīm b. Mūsā, alias Kāstrū, to be his agent (*wakīl*).

411 (b) 10 Shawwāl, 944: As an agent for Kāstrū, the above-mentioned rented from the Ḥanafī kadi who serves as the *'imām* of The Dome of the Rock a plot of land (*sāḥa*) and a bridge (*majāẓ*) in the Inner Ṣahyūn quarter, approximately 160 x 160 *dhirā'*. Kāstrū's house borders this land on its east. The lease is for 100 years for 2,000 *'uthmānī* for the entire period, with a down payment of 160 *'uthmānī*. It was concluded in the presence of Muḥammad Chelebī *al-naqqāsh*[38] who approved of it, as did the Ḥanbalī and the Ḥanafī kadis.

467 (c) The last third (*awākhir*) of Jumādā'l-Awwal, 943: Yahūdā b. Isḥāq the Jew complained against Falāq b. Ḥayyim, the head (*shaykh*) of the Jewish community, who allegedly had stolen his blue headgear (*shadd*).

[38] On the role played by this Ottoman high official in the rebuilding of Jerusalem, see "The Walls of Jerusalem."

Volume 8
(1537 - 1538)

37 (d) 12 Jumādā'l-Ākhir, 944: Ibrāhīm b. Mūsā the Jew, serving as a tax collector in Nablus and its district, collected the road tax due from Christian pilgrims who came to visit Jerusalem.

42 (a) 24 Dhū'l-Qa'da, 944: Two Muslim *shaykhs* guaranteed the payment of the road tax (*khafar*) due from the Jewish pilgrims who arrived in Jerusalem from Damascus. This was a group of 24 European (*'ifranj*) Jews, men and women, as well as 21 other *musta'riba* Jews.

46 (c) 25 Dhū'l-Qa'da, 944: 128 Jewish pilgrims were reported to have come from Damascus and its vicinity (*al-bilād al-shāmiyya*) to Jerusalem via Nablus. 28 of them were Jerusalemites, hence not liable for *ghafar* road tax. The total sum collected was 4,600 *'uthmānī*, paid at the rate of 1 *qubruṣī* gold coin and 8 silver *qiṭ'a* per person. The Jew Isḥāq b. Ibrāhīm Kurduba and the Jew Isḥāq Talmar (?) collected it for the commander (*dizdār*) of the Jerusalem Citadel.

47 (d) 25 Dhū'l-Qa'da, 944: The Jew Ibrāhīm b. Sulaymān and Kidalyā paid the governor of Nablus the road tax due from the above-mentioned 37 Jewish pilgrims guaranteed by the two Muslim *shaykhs*. The rate paid was 1 *qubruṣī* gold coin plus 8 silver *qiṭ'a* per person the 7 Jerusalemites in the group were exempted.

59 (a) 27 Dhū'l-Qa'da, 944: The Jews agreed that the meat price for sheep would be 13 *dirham ḥalabiyya* per *raṭl*, and if it were 13 for the Muslims, the Jews would pay an additional *dirham*.

72 (b) 7 Dhū'l-Ḥijja, 944: Nasīm b. Shū'ā the Jew brought a charge against Sa'īd b. Tamām the Jew whom he held responsible as an authorized agent (*wakīl*) of his son Hārūn for the *nafaqa* maintenance payment the latter

owed his divorced wife in accordance with her Hebrew language marriage contract (2,000 *'uthmānī*).

81 (c) 11 Dhū'l-Ḥijja, 944: Nasīm b. Mūsā b. Shabtūn the North African Jew admitted that he had given his daughter Ḍarīfa in marriage to Hārūn b. Sa'īd for a bride price of 4,000 *'uthmānī*, of which he actually received 2,000.

81 (e) 11 Dhū'l-Ḥijja, 944: In the Hebrew language marriage contract of Hārūn b. Sa'īd it was agreed that half of the bride price to the amount of 5,000 *ḥalabiyya* will be given to the bride's father, and the second half will be deferred (*mu'ajjal*), as usual.

120 (a) 24 Dhū'l-Ḥijja, 944: The Jewish community of Jerusalem was permitted to slaughter only on Thursdays and Mondays. As a result of complaints of sales of Jewish slaughtered meat to Muslims, they were forbidden to do so under threat of a 1,000 *'uthmānī* fine to The Dome of the Rock.

171 (b) 7 Muḥarram, 945: Tāj al-Dīn al-Sukkarī acknowledged receipt of all the payments on account of "the fifty days tax" (*'ādat al-khams īn*) from the Jewish silversmiths to the amount of 600 *ḥalabiyya* per year. Nasīm the Jewish silversmith and a Christian silversmith testified to this effect.

253 (a) 2 Ṣafar, 945: Three Muslims pledge to Mūsā b. *ḥaddād*, Faraj-Allah, and Ya'qūb Falāq as authorized agents for the Jewish community, that they will undertake the protection of the Jewish quarter for the monthly sum of 1 *qubruṣī* gold coin to each of them.

328 (b) 1 Rabī' al-Awwal, 945: A Jewish woman, Ḥannā b. Yahūdā, the wife of 'Abd al-Karīm the tanner (*adamī*) was returning home from "the Sultan's pool" where she had been washing her laundry when a Muslim stopped her, asked whether she was Jewish, then hit her with a stone and wounded her head.

341 (b) 5 Rabī' al-Awwal, 945: Yahūda b. Mūsā, the Jewish money changer of the *waqf* of the Temple Mount

guaranteed the Jew Yūsif b. Sulaymān to the *ṣūbāshī* of Jerusalem.

354 (a) 8 Rabī' al-Awwal, 945: Mināḥīm b. Zaqīlmān the Jew was accused by the *muḥtasib* of the sale of salt at the price of 2 *dirham* per *raṭl*, which is one-half *dirham* more than the official price.

378 (d) The first third (*awā'il*) of Jumādā'l-Ākhir, 945: The Jewish community complained to the authorities in Istanbul that they were being stopped from slaughtering meat and from building houses. A decree confirms their right to perform those activities and forbids the *muḥtasib* from entering the spice dealers' market or molesting them in any manner.

Volume 9
(1540)

72-73[39] The first third (*awā'il)* of Jumādā'l-Ākhir, 947: A Sultanic decree (*firmān*) issued in Istanbul and addressed to the governors and judges residing in the various urban centres of the province of Damascus. It forbids any attempt–such as was actually reported from Safed–of the Jewish communities (and other nonbelievers) to build new places of worship other than the old synagogues. This decree reiterates an earlier order to this effect and is applicable even in cases of real estate purchased or lawfully rented by the Jews.

[39] Turkish.

Volume 10
(1538 - 1539)

68 (b) 14 Jumādā'l-Awwal, 945: The Jew Mūsā b. Faraj Allah presented the court with a document (dated *awā'il* Ramaḍān, 940) issued by the *daftardār* of Damascus forbidding the *muḥtasib* of Jerusalem from entering the spice dealers' market, forcing them to purchase soap or any other commodity, or molesting them in any possible manner.

170 (a) 10 Rajab, 945: The following Jews guaranteed (*kafāla*) their coreligionists to the *ṣūbāshī* of Jerusalem: Ya'qūb Falāq (the head of the community), Faraj-Allah Baqbūq, Faraj-Allah al-Jawjarī, Mūsā b. Zaqilmān, 'Azrā, Barakāt, Sa'dya, Shiḥāta, and Mūsā. The head (*shaykh*) of the al-Sharaf quarter guaranteed them too.

191 (c) 24 Jumādā'l-Ākhir, 945: Yahūdā b. Mūsā the Jewish money changer of the Two Exalted *Waqfs* (of the Temple Mount and of Hebron) received from the comptroller (*nāẓir*) of the *waqfs* the sum of 2,354 *'uthmānī* spent on them in the year 943.

328 (c) 28 Sha'bān, 945: Yūsif, the Maltese Jew, complained against a Muslim who had hit him and wounded his face. The defendant admitted to having done so and was sentenced to flogging (*ta'zīr).*

393 (c) 29 Ramaḍān, 945: A list of millers, including, among others: Shmū'īl the Jew, Abū 'Aṣaba the Jew, and Abū Dānī the Jew.

453 (c) 28 Shawwāl, 945: The taxes due from the village of Mikhmās for the year 945, in the amount of 7,500 *'uthmānī*, would be collected in two installments: one half within 4 months, the other 4 months later, with the authorization of Ya'īsh b. Farḥān, the Jewish tax collector (*multazim*) of the Imperial Domain (*khāṣṣ-i shāhī)* revenues.

458 (d) 27 Shawwāl, 945: *Al-mu'allim* Yūsif b. Shū'ā, the Jewish *multazim* of the districts of Gaza, Ramla, Jerusalem, and Hebron presented an order of the *daftardār* of Damascus that he go to Safed and hand over to the treasury his pledge for all taxes due for the following three years in the amount of 100,000 *'uthmānī*. Several Jews from Gaza and Jerusalem guaranteed him, pledging that if he could not deliver this sum they would personally do so.

464 (c) 28 Shawwāl, 945: *Al-mu'allim* Shamīla b. Sa'īd the Jew from Gaza leased the collection of the road tax (*ghafar*) of Jerusalem for 16 months.

465 (a) 28 Shawwāl, 945: As per the above. The sum involved is 10,700 *'uthmānī*.

466 (b) 29 Shawwāl, 945: The above Shamīla was arrested for nonpayment of the road tax he owed the high-ranking tax collector (*amīn*)[40] who had appointed him.

550 (a) 4 Dhū'l-Ḥijja, 945: The court investigated the allegation that several items had been stolen from the Franciscan monks of Dayr Ṣahyūn. Isḥāq b. Isḥāq, Yūsif b. Mūsā, and Mūsā b. Yahūda were Jewish interpreters present, together with a Christian interpreter.

---

[40] See *Population and Revenue*, p. 44.

Volume 11
(1591)

86[41] The first third *(awā'il)* of Sha'bān, 999: A Sultanic decree issued in Istanbul and addressed to both the governor and the judge of Jerusalem. The Jewish community residing in Jerusalem sent a petition to the Sultan requesting his intervention to put an end to attempts of the local Muslim authorities to levy unauthorized fines. This was done upon the false allegation that they turned some of their houses into formal places of worship, and although they lived in a Jewish neighborhood they were also accused of raising their voices in prayer and thus disturbing the Muslims at their prayers. An undated legal opinion *(fatwā)*[42] is appended to the decree ruling that Jewish worship of God and reading of the Torah should not be interrupted by the authorities as long as they do not raise their voices in public.

[41] Turkish.

[42] See U. Heyd, "Some Aspects of the Ottoman Fetva" in *Bulletin of the School of Oriental and African Studies* 32 (1969): 35-56.

Volume 12
(1540 - 1541)

92 (c) 21 Dhū'l-Ḥijja, 946: A clay vessel full of Mamluk copper coins was found in the Jewish quarter near the slaughterhouse in the course of the inspection of the foundations of the city walls.

128 (d) 1 Muḥarram, 947: *Al-mu'allim* Ya'īsh b. Farḥān, the Jew in charge of the collection of the imperial revenues (*khāṣṣ*) claimed that a Muslim master declared the manumission of his slave just before his death, hence the latter should now be regarded as a free Muslim.

149 (a) 5 Muḥarram, 947: Taxes for the year 947 due to the Imperial Treasury, other than those recorded in the *taḥrīr* register,[43] were collected through Ya'īsh the Jew, and they included the road tax (*ghafar*) levied from Jews and Christians, taxes on all goods imported to Jerusalem (except for wheat and barley), and tax on cotton.

263 (b) 16 Ṣafar, 947: Muslim butchers testified that Jewish slaughtering of sheep, if they are *qūshīr*, is entirely sold to the Jews; if it becomes *ṭrayf*, they hang it in the Jewish quarter and there sell it to any bidder–but do not sell it in the market.

313 (b) 2 Rabī' al-Awwal, 947: A Jewish tailor, *al-mu'allim* Ilyās b. Mūsā, was commissioned by the governor of the Jerusalem district to make him two shirts. He claimed to have carried out his assignment, while the governor accused him of fraud.

354 12 Ramaḍān, 946: Lead tiles were stolen from the roof of al-Aqṣā Mosque. A Hebronite glass maker, when questioned as to the origin of lead found at his disposal, claimed to have bought it from a Jewish spice dealer (*'aṭṭār*) in Jerusalem, named Sa'dyā.

---

[43] For the use of this term and the institution, see *Population and Revenue*, pp. 3-18.

405 (d) 4 Rabīʿ al-Ākhir, 947: Saʿīd b. Tamān the Jew admitted having sold food products at a price 70 percent higher than the official one.

433 13 Rabīʿ al-Ākhir, 947: A general description of the boundaries of the al-Jismāniyya endowment.[44]

502 (c) 21 Rajab, 947: The Jewish community of Jerusalem was accused of having introduced changes into their synagogue and its surroundings. The heads of the community–Falāq, Mūsā *al-dayyān*, Yūsif al-Jawjalī and Mūsā b. Shulāl–claimed that all these innovations had been authorized by the governor through the good offices of Ibrāhim Kastrū "the convert to Islam" (*al-muhtadī*).

509 (a) 24 Rajab, 947: A rough draft of the above accusation.

689 (c) 27 Ramaḍān, 947: Saʿīd b. Tamān the Jew owed another Jew, Hārūn b. Naḥḥās, 510 *ḥalabiyya* as rent for his house for 7 consecutive years.

---

[44] On the history of this important endowment, see Mujīr al-Dīn al-Ḥanbalī, *Al-Uns al-Jalīl bi-Taʾrīkh al-Quds waʾl-Khalīl*, vol. 2, p. 41. See also J. W. Hirschberg, "Ottoman Rule in Jerusalem in the Light of Firmans and Shariʿa Documents–Preliminary Note" in *Israel Exploration Journal* 11 (1952): 237-248.

Volume 13
(1541)

70 (a) 14 Dhū'l-Qa'da 947: Ya'qūb Falāq, the head of the Jewish community, Yūsif b. Ibrāhīm the Jewish *dayyān* and Mūsā Zaqīlmān the Jew asked and received the kadi's permission to arrest a spice dealer of their community (Sa'dūn b. Murdakhān) who allegedly went out of his mind, insulting and molesting his fellow Jews.

243 (d) 13 Muḥarram, 948: *Al-mu'allim* Ya'īsh b. Farḥān the Jew in charge of the collection of all imperial revenues acknowledged receipt of taxes due from several uninhabited villages (*mazra'a*) to the amount of 200 *'uthmānī.*

249 (a) 29 Muḥarram, 948: Butchers and meat supply.[45]

250 (c) 29 Muḥarram, 948: Moneylending among the butchers, including the Jewish ones (Ḥasūna b. Zurayk).

251 29 Muḥarram, 948: Detailed transactions and debts within the butchers' guild.

382 (a) 27 Rabī' al-Awwal, 948: A Christian convert to Islam.

383 (d) End of Rabī' al-Awwal, 948: The Jewish and Christian silversmiths complained to the Secretary of the Revenues of the Empire (*kātib al-wilāyāt... al-islāmiyya*) of an unlawful tax of 600 *'uthmānī* levied from them annually. Upon inspection of the *taḥrīr* register he forbade any similar levy.

398 (a) 9 Rabī' al-Ākhir, 948: Ya'qūb b. Ḥayyim, alias Falāq, the head of the Jewish community, rented from a Mālikī endowment a large complex (*ḥawsh*),[46] partly ruined, in the vicinity of the slaughterhouse. The 1,000

---

[45] See *Economic Life*, pp. 18-60.

[46] See A. Raymond, *Grandes villes arabes a l'epoque ottomane* (Paris, 1985), pp. 323-325.

'uthmānī rent due for the 30 years lease will be spent by the lessee on repairs of the building.

458 (b) 18 Rabī' al-Ākhir, 948: The annual tax owed to the Sultan's treasury (*khāṣṣ*) from the revenues of al-Jab'a uninhabited villages (*mazra'a*) near the village of Sārīs, 1,500 *'uthmānī* for the year 947, is due from Ya'īsh the Jewish tax collector (*'āmil*), acting in the service of the district governor of Jerusalem and his deputy.

461 (a) 29 Rabī' al-Ākhir, 948: The above-mentioned Ya'īsh is in charge of tax collection from the entire district of Jerusalem. He received from the governor's deputy 500 *'uthmānī*, the rest to be collected later.

500 (a) 14 Jumādā'l-Awwal, 948: 'Abd-Allāh b. Isrā'īl, a Jewish carpenter in Jerusalem had invited Yūnis b. Sha'bān, a Jew from Aleppo, to stay in his house and even married him to Marḥabā the Jewish woman. Now 'Abd-Allāh accused Yūnis of having stolen a certain garment from his own house.

Volume 14
(1541 - 1542)

65 (b) 26 Sha'bān, 948: The Monastery of the Cross suffers from natural disasters and human vandalism.

98 (b) 10 Ramaḍān, 948: *Al-mu'allim* Mūsā, the Jewish money changer (*ṣayrafī*) presented the court with a Sultanic *berāt*[47] document (dated 21 Sha'bān, 944) appointing him money changer of the Manṣūrī *ribāṭ*[48] in Jerusalem for which service he will be entitled to a daily salary of one *'uthmānī*.

113 (a) 16 Ramaḍān, 948: *Al-mu'allim* Yūsif b. Shū'a, the Jewish tax collector (*'āmil*) of the Sultanic revenues in Gaza "and elsewhere" owes the kadi of Ramla 6,800 *'uthmānī* 2,400 for a loan the kadi had given him, 4,400 for two gold bracelets and a gold chain weighing 45 *mithqāl* the kadi sold him.

120 (b) 10 Jumādā'l-Awwal, 948: Yūsif b. Shū'a, the Jewish tax collector did the actual investigation and registration (*taftīsh wa-taḥrīr*) of the different entries in the *taḥrīr* register estimate (*takhmīn*) and the actual villages and other sources that owed taxes to the imperial treasury under the jurisdiction of the district governor of Jerusalem–25,200 *'uthmānī* for 947 (end of document missing).

126 (a) 20 Ramaḍān, 948: The taxes due from several villages in the subdistrict (*nāḥiya*) of Jerusalem for the year 945 amount to 2,600 *'uthmānī*. The Jewish collector, *al-mu'allim* Yūsif b. Dānyāl, had sent in 2,000 through *al-mu'allim* 'Āzir b. Murdakhāy and *al-mu'allim* Yūsif, both Jewish, and now paid the remaining 600.

135 (a) 24 Ramaḍān, 948: Tāj al-Dīn al-Sukkarī bought from *al-mu'allim* Yūsif b. Shū'a, the former tax collector

---

[47] On this term, *EI*^{2}, s.v. "Berāt."
[48] *EI*, s.v. "Ribāṭ."

(*'āmil*) of revenues of the imperial treasury, 4,000 *'uthmānī* worth of grains left by the deceased *tīmār* holder of Yālū, in the subdistrict (*nāḥiya*) of Ramle.

136 (a) 25 Ramaḍān, 948: Yūsif ibn Shū'a, the Jewish tax collector (blurred copy illegible).

142 (d) 28 Ramaḍān, 948: A Muslim owes Yahūda the money changer some money.

264 (d) 29 Dhū'l-Qa'da, 948: Christian and Jewish silversmiths (the latter: Ibrāhīm b. Faraj-Allāh, Nasīm b. Sabtūn, Ya'qūb) pledged to conduct all their professional activity (purchase and sale of silver, production) in *sūq al-sulṭān* market only.

291 (b) 12 Dhū'l-Ḥijja, 948: The head of the Jewish community, Falāq, as well as a few other Jews asked the court to arrest Sa'dūn the Jew who "has a defect in his mind" and therefore attacks fellow Jews and causes trouble to the community.

304 (f) 19 Dhū'l-Ḥijja, 948: The *ṣūbāshī* brought to court Falāq, head of the Jewish community, and his wife, and a few items (e.g.: white and black *shadd* silk cloth) that she allegedly had stolen from al-'Ayn bathhouse. Falāq explained that these had been mixed up in their belongings.

336 (a) End of Dhū'l-Ḥijja, 948: Ya'qūb Falāq, the head of the Jewish community, accused Dā'ūd b. Ḥayyim the Jew of having assaulted him. When the defendant denied it a Muslim and a Jewish witness were brought to the court and their testimony was accepted as sufficient proof.

408 (a) 24 Muḥarram, 949: 5 Jews from Safed (names given) pledged to pay 1,240 *'uthmānī* to a Muslim who would escort them on their way from Safed to Jerusalem.

409 (b) 28 Muḥarram, 949: The *'imām* of The Dome of the Rock accused Ya'qūb Falāq, the head of the Jewish community of unlawful possession of a house in the Ṣahyūn quarter near the slaughterhouse (and the Manṣūri soap factory), which he alleged was part of an

endowment under his supervision. The Jew claimed to have rented it from a Muslim official, but the kadi declared the rental void and ordered the Jew to vacate the premises.

421 (b) 28 Muḥarram, 949: The money that Tāj al-Dīn al-Sukkarī had originally been allowed by Yūsif b. Shū'a the Jewish tax collector (*'āmil*) to pay for the grain of the late *tīmār* holder of Yālū, is to be actually paid–with the permission of the above Yūsif–to the officer in charge of the janissary garrison of the citadel of Hebron.

434 (b) End of Muḥarram, 949: Bayram b. Shū'ā, the Jewish tax collector of the imperial revenues collection authorized the transfer of the taxes collected from a village nearby to a janissary stationed in the Jerusalem Citadel.

436 (b) 1 Ṣafar, 949: A Muslim testifies that he is authorizing the Jewish physician, Ibrāhīm b. Shūmal, also present in court, to treat him with any medication he chooses, and should any harm befall him, the doctor will not be held responsible for it.

439 (a) 2 Ṣafar, 949: The taxes due for the year 948 from the uninhabited village (*mazra'a*) called Jab'a which was part of the village of Sā rīs, were officially registered in the name of Ya'īsh b. Farḥān the Jew. He acknowledged receipt of 800 *'uthmānī* and is still entitled to 500.

444 (d) 2 Ṣafar, 949: The *tīmār* holder of the village of Sammū' who was absent from his village on official duty in the Ḥawrān is entitled to take possession now of the taxes collected from the village during his absence by the Jewish tax collector, Yūsif b. Shū'a.

458 (b) 6 Ṣafar, 949: A detailed list of the outstanding debts of the governor of Jerusalem to the imperial treasury (37,000 *'uthmānī*), already paid in part to the janissaries of the Citadel upon the authorization of Yūsif b. Shū'a the tax collector.

458 (c) 6 Ṣafar, 949: A village near Yālū (Ramla district), originally part of a *tīmār*, was leased by one of the

Jerusalem governor's people with the permission of Yūsif b. Shū'a.

460 (a) 6 Ṣafar, 949: *Al-mu'allim* Yūsif b. Shū'a will collect all the dues of a *tīmār* holder during his absence in the service of the Sultan.

460 (b) 6 Ṣafar, 949: Yūsif b. Mūsā, the *'ifranjī* ("European") Jewish taylor, and Aṣlān b. Frāyim the Jew guaranteed a Christian *'ifranjī* (Catholic) debtor for the substantial sum of 162 gold coins.

461 (a) 6 Ṣafar, 949: Mūsā b. Dā'ūd b. Ya'qūb the Rabbanite Jew from Mosul(?) established an endowment (*waqf*) of a house he had bought in the al-Sharaf quarter (formerly the al-Akrād quarter) on 29 Dhū'l-Ḥijja, 925. Detailed.

496 (d) 20 Ṣafar, 949: Tāj al-Dīn al-Sukkarī and Muḥammad b. Zurayq leased the *ghafar* road taxes to be levied at the gates of Jerusalem for one whole year for the total amount of 7,000 *'uthmānī*.

749 (d) 12 Jumādā'l-Awwal, 949: The Jewish spice dealer Yūsif admitted having sold candles at a price 10 percent higher than the official price.

Volume 15
(1543)

91 (d) 26 Ramaḍān, 949: Barūkh b. Mudkhīl Kūhīn (Cohen), the Jewish painter, representing Isḥāq b. Yūsif the Jew, authorized the head builder of Jerusalem to reconstruct the dilapidated wall of the monastery (*dayr*) of the Jews known as *al-aman*[49] (lit.: German, i.e. Ashkenazi).

181 (c) 15 Dhū'l-Qa'da, 949: Falāq, the head of the Jewish community, and the community's rabbi (*dayyān*), declared that they will not conduct any marriage without a specific permit of the kadi.

211 (a) 2 Dhū'l-Ḥijja, 949: Ya'qūb b. Yūsif and Yūsif b. Ibrāhīm, Jerusalemite Jews, undertook to transfer all the taxes (*'awāriḍ*) collected in the towns and subdistricts of Jerusalem and Hebron. They will be held responsible for any defective gold or silver coins. For their toil they will be remunerated 600 *'uthmānī*.

312 (a-e) 24 Rajab, 950: The Aleppo Jew, Sum'a b. Nāṣir, now living in Jerusalem, divorced his wife "a triple divorce" (i.e. a final one, according to Muslim jurisprudence). The divorced wife declares that she has not married anyone else, her former husband does not owe her anything, and she will take exclusive charge of her five-year-old daughter.

313 (a-b) 24 Rajab, 950: The Jewess Sanīna b. Mikhā'īl guaranteed her son Yūsif, and both he and his wife (the above-mentioned divorcée) mutually guaranteed one another that they would not marry anyone else.

333 (b) 1 Ṣafar, 950: Yūsif the Jewish *dayyān*, and Ya'qūb Falāq the head of the Jewish community, declared that they would like the above-mentioned Sanīna, her son

---

[49] For the use of this term in Ottoman official documents, see *Population and Revenue*, pp. 158-160.

Yūsif, and her daughter-in-law b. al-Munnā to continue living in the Jewish quarter of Jerusalem.

335 (d) 2 Rajab, 950: The *muḥtasib* of Jerusalem agreed with the Jewish community and its *dayyān*, Yūsif, that the latter would slaughter for his community on any day and at any place he chooses as long as he stays in town, and if absent, the Jewish community will choose someone else to replace him. If he slaughters an animal and the meat becomes *'iṭreyf* it will be sold in the market called *sūq al-sulṭān*.

341 (c-d) 6 Ṣafar, 950: Bayram b. Shū'a, as an authorized agent of his brother Yūsif, the Jewish tax collector, demanded that a Catholic monk from the Dayr Ṣahyūn monastery pay him the road tax (*ghafar*) due from the 46 pilgrims, at the rate of 14 *qiṭ'a* per person (7 each way). To support his claim, Bayram presented a document from the *sijill* of Ramla authorizing the levy of 14 *qiṭ'a* from each Georgian pilgrim.[50]

341 (e) 6 Ṣafar, 950: Sulaymān b. Yūsif, the North African Jew, demanded that 'Azīza b. Sulaymān, the Jewish North African woman, pay the 3 gold coins her husband owed him since Ṣafar, 948.

341 (f) 6 Ṣafar, 950: Sa'dya b. Yahūda and Sa'īd b. Ya'qūb, the Jewish spice dealers, acquitted the above-mentioned woman from the above-mentioned debt.

350 (c) Another copy of 341 (c-d).

394 (a) 5 Rabī' al-Awwal, 950: The head (*shaykh*) of the al-Sharaf quarter complained that the house of Yūsif b. Mūsā the Jew in that quarter was broken into during the night and a few of his belongings were stolen.

401 (d) 8 Rabī' al-Awwal, 950: A Muslim guard pledged himself responsible to the head of the Jewish community for anything that might be stolen from the al-Rīsha quarter.

---

[50] See *Population and Revenue*, pp. 58, 70-72.

451 (c) 29 Rabīʿ al-Awwal, 950: Yaʿqūb Falāq, the head of the Jewish community, pledged to refrain from slaughtering full-grown (*kibār*) sheep without specific permission of the Muslim butchers.

465 (f) 8 Rabīʿ al-Ākhir, 950: Falāq, the head of the Jewish community, pledged to refrain from performing any marriage without the kadi's permission.

498 (b) 19 Rabīʿ al-Ākhir, 950: When accused of embezzlement of public revenues the Jewish *ʿāmil* Yūsif b. Shūʿa, was warned by the district governor of Jerusalem that he should collect only taxes due to him.

Volume 16
(1544 - 1545)

133 (d) 27 Sha'bān, 951: The Jews Yūsif b. Shlūmū and Isḥāq b. Hārūn rented one third of a house in the Jewish quarter (near the bakery) and spent 110 *ḥalabiyya* on repairs.

147 (g) 5 Ramaḍān, 951: Ḥabūba the Jewish woman was accused of having sold white sugar using deficient weights.

203 (a) 10 Shawwāl, 951: Khalīfa the Jew was accused by the inspector of the markets (*muḥtasib*) of the sale of meat to Rufā'īl the Jew using deficient weights.

236 (a) 27 Shawwāl, 951: Muslim vendors of meat pledge themselves to refrain from the sale of Jewish slaughtered meat to the Muslims or from its introduction into the market (*sūq*).

249 (c) 1 Dhū'l-Qa'da, 951: Jawhara b. Hārūn, the Jewish woman, complained about her husband Ibrāhīm who did not provide her with money nor did he live with her any more.

354 (b) End of Dhū'l-Ḥijja, 951: A key to one of the gates of the walls of Jerusalem was found with "the robbers." Upon an order of the governor of Damascus to investigate among the blacksmiths, the Jewish members of this guild, Ḥabīb b. Shmū'īl and Sāsī b. Ibrāhīm were interrogated and found not guilty.

403 (d) 18 Muḥarram, 952: The Jew Ya'īsh b. Farḥān confirms that a certain Muslim will collect the revenues of several villages in the Hebron and Jerusalem subdistricts for the year 951.

416 (d) 22 Muḥarram, 952: Ya'īsh b. Farḥān grants the former *muḥtasib* Tāj al-Dīn al-Sukkarī the right to collect the

imperial revenues due from several villages for the year 951.

418 (a) 22 Muḥarram, 952: Ya'qūb Falāq, the head of the Jewish community, paid the poll tax (*kharāj*) due from the community for the year 952–85 *sulṭānī* gold coins.

502 (b) End of Ṣafar, 952: Arṣlān b. Ibrāhīm the Jew complained that Mūsā b. Ismā'īl the Jew had beaten him.

542 (b) 21 Rabī' al-Awwal, 952: A tīmār holder who allegedly owes 2,600 *'uthmānī* in tax arrears for the year 945 issues receipts for the payment of 2,000 to the Jewish tax collectors (*multazim*) Yūsif and Ya'īsh, and an exemption order from the governor of Damascus on account of his participation in the Baghdad war, and belated payment when he returned therefrom.

Volume 17
(1545 - 1546)

36 (b) 19 Rabīʻ al-Thānī, 952: Shiḥāda, Būbūz, Mūsā *al-'ifranjī,* ʻAbd al-Kalīm, and his son Ibrāhīm–all Jews–bought 21 water buffalo hides from the kadi of Jerusalem. Yaʻqūb Falāq, the head of the Jewish community, guaranteed their debt.

107 (a) 21 Jumādā'l-Awwal, 952: A Jerusalemite Jew bought a house in Cairo (Bāb Zuwayla quarter) for 10,000 *ʻuthmānī*. A detailed description of the house.

162 (c) 16 Jumādā'l-Thānī, 952: Ibrāhīm b. Mūsā, the Rabbanite Ashkenazi (*alāmanī*) Jew, bought a vegetable garden (*ḥākūra*) from two Muslims, (including the ruins of a building) to its north is the Jew Mūsā Shulāl's house. The sale was concluded for 12 gold coins (end of document missing).

285 (a) 19 Shaʻbān, 952: Khusraw, the Muslim official sent to collect the taxes due to the imperial treasury received from Bayram b. Shūʻa the Jewish *ʻāmil* 4,000 *dirham* on account of villages and *mazraʻas* in the Hebron area.

297 (c) 25 Shaʻbān, 952: The butchers' guild; meat supply to Jerusalem; complaints of *sipāhīs.*

300 (a-b) 27 Shaʻbān, 952: The Muslim high-ranking official (*amīn)* in charge of the taxes for the imperial treasury received from the Jewish *ʻāmil* in the Jerusalem district, Bayram b. Shūʻa, the sum of 90 gold coins on account of revenues for the year 951.

310 (e) 3 Ramaḍān, 952: The sale of a few belongings (text somewhat blurred) of the wife of the Jew Yaʻīsh by the latter's Jewish servant (*khidmatkār*) is cancelled since the owner disapproved of it.

319 (f) 8 Ramaḍān, 952: A Jewish woman, Anā b. Yaʻqūb, was accused by the *muḥtasib* and found guilty of the sale of

kmāj unleavened bread using deficient weights (a *raṭl* was one *'uqiyya* short).

336 (f) 17 Ramaḍān, 952: The Jewish miller al-Zalabānī was brought to court by the *muḥtasib* who accused him of selling flour to another Jew at an inflated price: 5 *ḥalabiyya* per *mudd* instead of the official rate of 4.

469 (b) 3 Dhū'l-Ḥijja, 952: Shemṭūb b. Ya'qūb, the Jewish tax collector (*'āmil*) in charge of the imperial treasury revenues in the Jerusalem and Gaza districts authorized the Jew Yūsif b. Shū'a to be his agent and to represent him in all his financial and other public activities.

472 (c) 4 Dhū'l-Ḥijja, 952: The widow of a *sipāhī* came to court accompanied by Shemṭūb b. Ya'qūb, the Jewish *'āmil*, who had provided her with a receipt for payments made out of her husband's belongings. Now she insists on collecting a substantial amount allegedly due to her.

477 (a) 7 Dhū'l-Qa'da, 952: Khusraw, the Muslim high-ranking official (*amīn*) in charge of the collection of the imperial taxes in the Jerusalem district, accompanied by the Jewish tax collector (*'āmil*) in the Gaza and Jerusalem districts, Shemṭūb b. Ya'qūb, as well as Isḥāq b. Yūsif, the Jewish money changer (*ṣayrafī*) declared in court that he cancelled the lease (*muqāṭa'a*)[51] of several villages (one of which had been leased by Isḥāq) for the year 951.

477 (c) 7 Dhū'l-Qa'da, 952: Khusraw, accompanied by Shemṭūb the Jew, declared the cancellation of another *muqāṭa'a* lease, this time to a *sipāhī*, who had paid all his dues for 951.

585[52] (a) The first third (*awā'il*) of Rabī' al-Ākhir, 952: A Sultanic decree addressed to the judge of Jerusalem and based on a petition sent by the Jews under his jurisdiction. The local authorities levied unlawful penalties from them when they wanted to repair houses that they legally owned (*mulk*). The judge was ordered to investigate the factual background of this complaint

---

[51] See *Population and Revenue*, p. 162, n. 24.

[52] Turkish.

and if it was found valid, such behavior should immediately be discontinued. Any insubordination should be reported to Istanbul.

590[53] (a) 3 Dhū'l-Ḥijja, 942: A Sultanic decree from Istanbul to the kadi of Jerusalem based on a petition of the Jews residing there. When a member of their community died they were challenged by the officials in charge of heirless inheritances (*bayt al-māl*) to produce a Muslim witness. Failing that, their claim to the inheritance would not be accepted. The Sultan decreed that the judge should not permit any transgression of the Muslim *sharī'a* law even by the officials of *bayt al-māl*.

---

[53] Turkish.

Volume 18
(1546 - 1547)

8 (d) 18 Ṣafar, 953: The poll tax (*kharāj*) of the Christians of Jerusalem for the year 953 was levied by the official (*amīn*) in charge of the imperial treasury revenues and in the presence of Shemtūb, the Jewish tax collector (*'āmil*).

17 (a) 22 Ṣafar, 953: A delegation from Jerusalem is sent to the village of Taqū' to deal with the Haytham bedouins and buy bitumen[54] extracted from the Dead Sea. They buy 47 *qinṭārs* for 23,500 *'uthmānī*. The Jewish *'āmil*, Shemtūb, as part of the delegation, also stays in the village.

33 (b) 27 Ṣafar, 953: Ya'qūb Falāq, the head of the Jewish community, borrowed 9 *qubruṣī* gold coins from the kadi for one month.

36 (b) 28 Ṣafar, 953: The Jew *al-khōja*[55] Yūsif b. Shū'a owed the Jew Ya'īsh b. Farḥān 100 *'uthmānī* due for 953 from several villages he leased. Ya'īsh acknowledged receipt of the entire sum.

52 (g) 8 Rabī' al-Awwal, 953: The Jewess Malīḥa b. Ibrāhīm, wife of Yūsif, the *'ifranjī* Jewish cloth merchant, authorized *khōja* Aṣlān b. Ibrāhīm, the Jewish cloth merchant to be in charge of a house she owned in the Jewish quarter, above the oil press.

57 (c) 8 Rabī' al-Awwal, 953: A janissary from the Hebron citadel gave the Jewish silversmith some silver and commissioned 2 pairs of earrings. Upon receipt of the final product he complains of some silver missing.

102 (e) End of Rabī' al-Awwal, 953: For the imperial treasury and in the name of the Muslim high official (*amīn*) in

---

54 *Op. cit.*, p. 59, n. 42.

55 The more prevalent spelling is *khawāja*. Cf. *Jewish Life*, pp. 145, 184, 214.

charge of imperial treasury revenues and the Jewish local tax collector (*'āmil*), Sulaymān, a Muslim levied the taxes due from the village of Kafr 'Aqib for 952.

207 (d) 25 Jumādā'l-Awwal, 953: A Jewish woman, Qamar, converted to Islam in court. Details of her formal declaration.

207 (e) 25 Jumādā'l-Awwal, 953: The above-mentioned marries a Muslim in court.

267 (b) 22 Jumādā'l-Ākhira, 953: Yahūdā b. Mūsā the money changer was authorized by his brother-in-law, the Jew Yūsif "the trader in salt" (*mallāḥ*) for the lease of the taxes of the village al-Ṭīra for 953. Signatures of Jewish witnesses (*shuhūd al-ḥāl*).

267 (c) 22 Jumādā'l-Ākhira, 953: The above-mentioned pays a Muslim debtor a debt on account of the above village taxes.

277 (b) The last third (*awākhir*) of Jumādā'l-Ākhir, 953: The Jew Yamṭūm b. Isḥāq was accused of the disappearance of a Christian named Paolo who was last seen in his house. He denied the allegation and was acquitted.

297 (a) The first third (*awā'il*) of Rajab, 953: Dā'ūd b. Shmū'īl b. Shūshān the Jew is appointed trustee for Ibrāhīm b. Isḥāq b. Ibrāhīm b. Nātān whose father was known as Shulāl or the Nagid (*al-nāghīd*). He is entitled to 25,000 *sulaymānī* silver coins from the Karaite *al-mu'allim* Ṣadaqa b. Yūsif b. 'Abd al-Wālī.

297 (b) The first third (*awā'il*) of Rajab, 953: In 938 the above-mentioned Dā'ūd bought from the above-mentioned Ṣadaqa a large house (and a mill located within it) in the al-Sharaf quarter for 100,000 *'uthmānī*. The mother of the above-mentioned orphan approached Dā'ūd and had him acknowledge having conducted this transaction for her son, whereupon the court confirmed it formally as her son's property.

298 (b) The first third of Rajab, 953: Two Muslim witnesses testified to the effect that in 930 the above-mentioned Ṣadaqa acknowledged that the above-mentioned Isḥāq

no longer owes him the sum of 100,000 *'uthmānī* which he had paid him in full.

304 (e) 14 Rajab, 953: A *sipāhī* testified that he owed Yaḥyā b. Isḥāq the Jew 36 gold coins he had lent him.

348 (a) 9 Sha'bān, 953: The Jewish money changer, Isḥāq b. Yūsif, acknowledged receipt of 537 *sulṭānī* gold coins for a variety of commercial transactions, detailed in the document.

491 (a) 23 Shawwāl, 953: Yahūdā b. Mūsā, the Jewish money changer sued a Muslim for a debt of 300 *ḥalabiyya* the latter allegedly owed him for 30 sheep he had bought. When the court found the Muslim guilty he cursed the Jew and declared that he would never pay, and if he ever did, "may he turn Jewish."

510 (e-f) 5 Dhū'l-Qa'da, 953: The Muslim who operated "the bathhouse of the Patriarch" (*ḥammām al-baṭrak*) was sentenced for having used unclean towels and was warned that he should provide clean but separate towels to the Muslims on the one hand, and to the Jews and Christians as well as the villagers on the other. The operator of the al-'Ayn bathhouse was also warned.

634 (d) 22 Muḥarram, 954: Ya'qūb Falāq, the head of the Jewish community, delivered the poll tax due from 85 people for the year 954.

Volume 19

(1547)

65 (a) 21 Rabīʿ al-Awwal, 954: Nūna b. Rūbīn, a Jewish woman, reached an agreement with the Muslim head of the North African (*maghāriba*) community allowing her to spend 2,145 *ḥalabiyya* on repairs of the house she rented from the North African *waqf* endowment in the Jewish quarter. She will, however, be exempted from 5 years rent.

105 (a) 9 Rabīʿ al-Ākhir, 954: Jewish members of the cobblers' guild–Shiḥāta b. Shamīla, Mūsā b. Ibrāhīm, Mūsā b. Salīm, and Yūsif b. Hānān–pledged to refrain from the use of dead animal hides.

106 (d) 10 Rabīʿ al-Thānī, 954: Mūsā b. Yūsif, the Jewish secretary (*kātib*) in charge of the income of the Imperial Domains in the districts of Jerusalem and Gaza acknowledged receipt of the road tax due from Jewish pilgrims to Jerusalem at the rate of 2 *qiṭʿa* per person: 40 *qiṭʿa* from Gazan and 120 from Damascene Jews.

108 (b) 10 Rabīʿ al-Thānī, 954: Yūsif b. Isḥāq, the *'ifranjī* Jewish cloth merchant, appointed Isḥāq b. Yūsif, the Jewish money changer as his trustee for the collection of all his dues from several Muslim high officials in Nablus and Jerusalem.

109 (b) 11 Rabīʿ al-Thānī, 954: A Muslim sold 10 *qinṭārs* of alkali to Isḥāq the Jew.

139 (b) 25 Rabīʿ al-Thānī, 954: An Ashkenazi Jewish person (*Askinājī al-yahūdā al-'ifranjī*) was accused by the inspector of the markets (*muḥtasib*) of the sale of *kaʿk* bread of a low quality and was cautioned that he should improve the quality of all his bread.

156 (b) 2 Jumādā'l-Awwal, 954: A very detailed list (including prices and quantities of items listed) of the inheritance

of the Jewish spice dealer, Faraj-Allah b. Khalīfa, alias al-Jawjalī, and its distribution to the various heirs.

170 (c) 6 Jumādā'l-'Ūlā, 954: The *muḥtasib* accused a Jewish merchant of the sale of inspissated juice of fruit (*rubb*) at an inflated price.

177 (c) 13 Jumādā'l-Awwal, 954: The Muslim head (*rayyis*)[56] of the physicians' guild of Jerusalem appointed a Christian and a Jewish deputy (the latter, "master" *al-rayyis* ʻAbd al-Karīm) for the duration of 8 months of his absence on a trip to the capital. The kadi confirmed.

273 (b) 6 Rajab, 954: A list of belongings of a deceased Jewish beautician (*kaḥḥāla*), Qamar b. Shmū'īl.

273 (d) 6 Rajab, 954: Although it was publicly announced (after complaints of the low quality of defective and copper coins reached the authorities) that only new coins (*fulūs*)[57] should be used, Yūsif the Jew was accused of using the old coins. He admitted his guilt and was flogged.

274 (c) 7 Rajab, 954: Two Jewish witnesses, Yahūdā the money changer and ʻAlī b. Sulaymān, testified that Yaʻqūb Falāq was appointed a trustee of the Jewish woman Dūnā.

311 (b) The last third of Rajab, 954: The al-ʻUmarī Mosque is located at the gate of the Jewish quarter, near the gate of the big marketplace (*al-sūq al-kabīr*).

321 (a) 28 Rajab, 954: A Muslim guarantees a debt of Yūsif b. Sulaymān the Jew.

337 (d) 5 Shaʻbān, 954: A sale of a house in al-Rīsha quarter adjacent to another house owned by Mūsā b. Shulāl the Jew.

---

[56] The term *rayyis* was often used in earlier years to designate physicians in general (Geoffrey Khan, *Arabic Legal and Administrative Documents in the Genizah Collections* [Cambridge, 1993], p. 250, n. 4).

[57] *EI*^{2}, s.v. "Fals."

356 (a) 11 Sha‘bān, 954: A detailed list of buyers of soap consignments from the inheritance of a deceased Muslim, among others: Jūkār the Jew, 60 *raṭls*, and Yūsif the Jewish sesame oil dealer (*sayrajānī*), 1 *qinṭār*.

395 25 Sha‘bān, 954: The Jew Ḥayyim b. Sulaymān claimed that he owned a certain building (details provided) in Damascus. He had been granted full possession of this building by its former owner, the rabbi (*dayyān*) of the Damascus Jewish community, Isḥaq b. Ya‘qūb. When full proof was submitted to the court the kadi ruled that neither the rabbi's widow nor her children have any rights in that building.

Volume 20
(1547 - 1548)

4 (b) 8 Shawwāl, 954: The chief builder of Jerusalem declares that no member of the Jewish community, including its head, Ḥayyim Falāq, owes him any money, except for a 300 *'uthmānī* debt of Falāq.

38 (c) 18 Shawwāl, 954: Yahūdā b. Mūsā the Jewish money changer acknowledged that he owed a Muslim 1 *qinṭār* of Jandali grapes from al-Māliḥa village.

115 (d) The last third of Dhū'l-Qa'da, 954: A Jewish physician, 'Abd al-Karīm b. Mūsā, rented his house in the Karaite Jewish quarter for a period of 4 years for the sum of 3,200 *'uthmānī* to a Muslim who undertook certain repairs in the building.

141 (d) The first third of Dhū'l-Ḥijja, 954: A list of 14 Jews (names provided) who died in Jerusalem of natural causes.

167-168 The last third of Dhū'l-Ḥijja, 954: An order was sent from Damascus to check the size of the Jewish community of Jerusalem for the preceding 5 years. Upon inspection the official in charge discovered 5 additional people, hence he levied a poll tax for 25 altogether, paid by Falāq, Ibrāhīm and Yūsif the *dayyān*.

236 (d) The last third of Muḥarram, 955: The Damascene Jewish silversmith Ya'īsh b. Yūsif, acknowledged receipt of 3,200 *'uthmānī* that his mother deposited with *al-mu'allim* Mūsā b. Ḥayyim Shulāl and Shmū'īl b. Sulaymān, the Jerusalemite Jews, in the year 948.

236 (e) The last third of Muḥarram, 955: The Jew Ibrāhīm b. Hārūn declared that if he did not return to his wife in Safed within 3 days he would be liable for a 2,000 *'uthmānī* fine to The Dome of the Rock.

317 (d) 10 Rabīʿ al-Awwal, 955: The special dry cheese prepared by the Jew al-Zalabānī is to be sold to Muslims for 5 *ʿuthmānī* per *raṭl*, and to the Jews for 6.

319 (b) 10 Rabīʿ al-Awwal, 955: The head of the North African (*shaykh al-maghāriba*) community rented a house located in the Jewish quarter to the Jewish woman Sāra b. Sīmūn for 3 years for the sum of 524 *ʿuthmānī*.

404 (c) 9 Rabīʿ al-Thānī, 955: The Jew Isḥāq b. Ibrāhīm rented a house in the Jewish quarter from a Muslim for 4 years.

547 (c) 27 Jumādā'l-Awwal, 955: A Muslim from the village of Qalūnya accused the Jew Shaʿshūʿ b. ʿĀzir of having unlawfully taken possession of an olive grove in the above village. The defendant proved that he had bought it in 939.

Volume 21
(1548 - 1549)

29 (c) 23 Jumādā'l-Ākhir, 955: Janissaries stationed in the Jerusalem Citadel acknowledge receipt of 169 *sulṭānī* gold coins from Yūsif, the Jewish tax collector (*'āmil*) of the imperial (*khāṣṣ*) revenues of Gaza, Ramla, and Hebron.

107 (b) 18 Rajab, 955: For 6 *sulṭānī* gold coins a Muslim buys from the North African Jew, Mas'ūd b. Ibrāhīm, 25 percent of an orchard (*ghirās*) of various trees (figs, vines, etc.) that Mas'ūd owns on the lands of al-'Āzariyya village, according to a purchase document issued in 925.

138 (a) 18 Rajab, 955: Two Muslim brothers own 50 percent of the partnership of an orchard in al-'Āzariyya village the other half was sold by their Jewish partners who owned it: Mas'ūd b. Ibrāhīm, Turkiyya b. 'Ammār, and Manūḥa b. Mūsā.

146 (b) 2 Sha'bān, 955: For the sum of 30 *sulṭānī* gold coins, a Muslim from the village of Bayt Sāḥūr al-Wād bought from the Jewish physician Yahūdā b. Mūsā b. Ya'qūb his share (25 percent) of an orchard he owned in accordance with a document issued in 927. 17 days later the entire deal was cancelled.

158 (b) 7 Sha'bān, 955: The Jew Mūsā b. Mūghān was hired by a cobbler for a period of one year, then fired by him after six months. The Jew demands his pay–5 *sulṭānī* gold coins–for the full year.

383 (b) 18 Dhū'l-Qa'da, 955: A Muslim builder demands his pay of 4 *qubruṣī* gold coins from the Jew Yahūdā b. al-Ṭalyānī who hired his services to reconstruct and repair parts of the house of al-Jawjalī.

383 (e) 19 Dhū'l-Qa'da, 955: The above-mentioned Jew paid the Muslim builder 3 gold coins on account of the

above-mentioned debt. He admitted that the remaining debt is 100 *ḥalabiyya*.

391 (a) 25 Dhū'l-Qa'da, 955: The poll tax (*kharāj*) due from the Jewish community of Jerusalem for the year 955 was received by the tax collector from Ya'qūb Falāq, the head of the Jewish community, for a total of 90 people (*nafar*).

464 (a) 3 Muḥarram, 956: An entry in the price list for food and other commodities: The *muḥtasib* will inspect the bathhouses daily to check their cleanliness and the supply of separate towels to the Muslims and the Jews and Christians (*al-dhimm*).

475 (a) 6 Muḥarram, 956: The Jew Mūsā Shulāl acknowledged a debt of 2,500 *ḥalabiyya* to a Muslim.

516 (e) 22 Muḥarram, 956: Isḥāq b. Yūsif, the Jewish money changer who used to be in the service of the former district governor of Jerusalem owes Tāj al-Dīn al-Sukkarī 100 *sulṭānī* gold coins in return for a loan extended to him.

517 (b) 24 Muḥarram, 956: Tāj al-Dīn al-Sukkarī, as reported by two Muslim dignitaries, approached the above-mentioned Isḥāq b. Yūsif by the entrance of the flour mill in front of the Jewish synagogue and demanded an accounting of what he did with the 20,000 *'uthmānī* he had given him. Yūsif confirmed their receipt adding that the entire sum was paid to the former governor, Sinān Pāshā.

542 (b) 4 Ṣafar, 956: A Muslim religious dignitary acknowledged receipt of 60 *sulṭānī* gold coins from Ya'qūb Falāq and from Mūsā Shulāl, who still owed him the sum of 20 more gold coins.

544 (c) 5 Ṣafar, 956: A Greek Orthodox tailor accused a Jewish tailor, Mūsā b. Ismā'īl, of having attacked him and cursed him publicly. The defendant denied the charge but when two Christian witnesses testified in support of the complaint, the Jew was found guilty and flogged.

Volume 22
(1549 - 1550)

4 (a) 27 Rabīʻ al-Awwal, 956: Yaʻqūb Falāq, the head of the Jewish community, was acquitted in an earlier case, when it transpired that he did not owe anything in conjunction with the pot (*dast*) he had allegedly taken from another Jew, *khōja* Yūsif, then found in the possession of Sabatya b. Mūsā the Jew.

6 (a) The last third of Rabīʻ al-Awwal, 956: Yūsif b. Shūʻa, the Jewish tax collector (*ʻāmil*) in the district of Jerusalem and Hebron, testified in the presence of the *ṣūbāshī*, representing the governor, that Yūsif had no outstanding debts or obligations whatsoever to the imperial treasury, and none to or from any functionary in conjunction with taxes formerly due.

112 14 Jumādā'l-'Ūlā, 956: A conflict between the Jewish community and a Muslim dignitary, Aḥmad al-Dajjānī,[58] as to the small building adjacent to the synagogue as well as to a mosque.

165 (c) 5 Jumādā'l-Thānī, 956: Isḥāq b. Antūn (?) the Jew asked for the court's permission to reconstruct the upper floor of a building in the Jewish quarter that belonged to the heirs of the Jew Ibrāhīm Kashtrū. After inspection by the chief builder permission was granted on condition that it be built precisely as it had been (7.5 x 4.5 x 3 *dhirāʻ*).

211 (c) 23 Jumādā'l-Thānī, 956: The Jew Yūsif b. Ibrāhīm the seasame oil dealer (*al-sayrajānī*) complained against the Jew Mūsā b. Ismāʻīl who allegedly had caused his arrest and the payment of a fine. Mūsā could not prove his claim that he had been provoked by Yūsif whereas the latter swore by God that he was telling the truth. Mūsā was convicted and flogged.

---

[58] For further references to him, see *Jewish Life*, pp. 77, 81, 93; U. Heyd, *Ottoman Documents*, pp. 149, 178. On earlier stages of this conflict, see Mujīr al-Dīn, vol. 2, pp. 300-314.

223 (d) 28 Jumādā'l-Thānī, 956: Isḥāq b. Sabtūn, the Jewish silversmith, pledged that he would never exercise his profession at home or any other place but the *Sūq al-Sulṭān* market.

251 (c) 11 Rajab, 956: The Jew Mūsā b. Shulāl accused a Muslim from Bayt Mazmīl village of having unlawfully kept for himself a cow which had actually been owned by the two of them in partnership.

332 (b) 18 Sha'bān, 956: The Jew Mūsā b. Zaqīlmān was accused by the *muḥtasib* of selling unbaked bread.

440 (b) 8 Shawwāl, 956: A Muslim dignitary acknowledged receipt of a 60 gold coin debt from Mūsā b. Shulāl, Ya'qūb Falāq, and Yaḥyā *al-dayyān.*

444 (b) 9 Shawwāl, 956: A Muslim silversmith declared in court that he was no longer entitled to any payment on account of two Hebrew language documents. The declaration is as follows: 66.5 gold coins for the sale of soap and 74 gold coins for a loan signed by the Jews Sa'dyā b. Yahūdā, Mūsā b. Shulāl, Sa'īd *al-Najjār,* Shmū'īl b. Sulaymān, Mūsā *a l-Bayḍānī,* Shabtay *al-gharābīlī,* and Yūsif *al-sayrajānī.*

447 (c) 10 Shawwāl, 956: A Jewish woman, Dūnā b. Ya'qūb, rented a house in the Jewish quarter from a Muslim dignitary for 5.5 years and for a rent of 26.5 *sulṭānī* gold coins, of which she may spend 1.5 gold coins on repairs.

489 (a) 29 Shawwāl, 956: A janissary accused Yūsif b. Shū'a, the Jewish tax collector (*'āmil*), of owing him 4 gold coins he had lent him. He could not produce any proof whereas the defendant took an oath on the Torah according to his religion.

495 (e) 1 Dhū'l-Qa'da, 956: The Jews Ibrāhīm b. 'Āzir and Isḥāq b. Ibrāhīm paid the entire debt of 40 gold coins they owed a Muslim for a load (*ḥiml*)[59] of soap.

[59] See *Economic Life,* pp. 88-89 and notes.

542 (c) 29 Dhū'l-Qa'da, 956: The scribe (*kātib*) for the imperial revenues–in the presence of *khawājā* Yūsif b. Shū'a, the Jewish tax collector (*'āmil*)–acknowledged receipt of the rent of several villages from their lessee.

559 (c) 11 Dhū'l-Ḥijja, 956: The Jews Sāsī b. Ibrāhīm and Ḥabīb b. Ibrāhīm pledged–in the presence of the head of the blacksmiths' guild (*ḥaddādī al-shams*)–to refrain from any further activity as blacksmiths in the villages of the district.

Volume 23
(1550)

3 (c) 19 Dhū'l-Ḥijja, 956: Ya'qūb, the Jewish physician, rented a "shop" (*dukkān*) from a Muslim endowment, then left Jerusalem and stopped paying his rent. By order of the kadi it was emptied of all its contents (a detailed list) and handed over to two other Jewish physicians, Mūsā and Shmu'āl.

16 (d) 25 Dhū'l-Ḥijja, 956: Ya'qūb, the head of the Jewish community, was appointed by the Jewish money changer, Yahūdā b. Mūsā, as his authorized agent (*wakīl*).

60 (b) 7 Muḥarram, 957: A Muslim from Yabrūd village claimed that a cow in the possession of the Jewish silversmith Ya'qūb b. Yūsif, belonged to him and was confiscated from al-Haytham bedouins by the governor of Nablus. The Jew admitted that it had been given to him by the governor, hence he was ordered to return it to its owner.

61 (b) 8 Muḥarram, 957: A janissary from the Jerusalem Citadel acknowledged receipt of a red cow and a young donkey he had deposited with the Jewish silversmith Ya'qūb b. Yūsif.

105 (f) 29 Muḥarram, 957: Sulaymān b. Isḥāq the Damascene Jewish *dayyān*, undertakes for himself as well as his community, to refrain in the future from constructing a new building without the specific permit of the kadi, and if he engaged an expert builder (*mu'allim*) he would pay him 6 *qiṭ'a* per day and half a *qiṭ'a* for his lunch.

144 (e) 17 Ṣafar, 957: The Jewish slaughterer, Ya'qūb b. Mūsā, pledged that he would only slaughter on Mondays and Thursdays.

146 (c) 21 Ṣafar, 957: Ya'qūb Falāq, the head of the Jewish community, paid the poll tax due from the Jews of Jerusalem for 956 for a total of 90 people (*nafar*).

273 (b) 3 Rabī' al-Thānī, 957: The official price of the cheese produced by the Jews was set at 20 *'uthmānī* for Jews, 18 *'uthmānī* for Muslims.

284 (b) 7 Rabī' al-Thānī, 957: The *muḥtasib* accused the Jew Mūsā b. Zaqīlmān of selling *kmāj* bread using a defective scale (details).

284 (d) 7 Rabī' al-Thānī, 957: The above-mentioned was also accused of the sale of bad-smelling bread.

365 (b) 6 Jumādā'l-Awwal, 957: A Muslim claims a debt of 4 gold coins from Ya'qūb Falāq, the head of the Jewish community.

369 (a) 8 Jumādā'l-'Ūlā, 957: A Muslim merchant bought from the Jew Ibrāhīm b. Faraj-Allah half of a house he owned in the al-Sharaf quarter in the street (*khaṭṭ*) of the Karaites for 25 gold coins. The other half of the house is owned by the Jewish silversmith Sa'ādāt b. Nassīm.

372 (b) 12 Jumādā'l-Awwal, 957: The cavalry officer (*sipāhī*) entitled to the tithe of the village of Silwān accused the heads of the Jewish community–Mūsā Shulāl, Sa'īd, Isḥāq, and Sulaymān–of burying their dead in a cave adjacent to the al-'Amrī Mosque. The kadi ordered that their dead be taken away.

372 (c) 11 Jumādā'l-Awwal, 957: A Muslim merchant is entitled to 2,500 *ḥalabiyya* from Sulaymān b. Shmu'īl the Jew for a transaction concerning cloth of various kinds Sulaymān had bought from him.

372 (d) 11 Jumādā'l-Awwal, 957: The above-mentioned Jew rented from the above-mentioned Muslim a shop located in the *sūq al-tujjār* market for one year for 600 *ḥalabiyya*.

374 (a) 12 Jumādā'l-'Ūlā, 957: The above-mentioned Sulaymān leased the above-mentioned shop to the Jew Ibrāhīm b.

Mīr for a year for 600 *ḥalabiyya*. The lessor authorized the lessee to dwell there.

398 (a) 22 Jumādā'l-Awwal, 957: The *ṣūbāshī* brought a group of Jews to court and reported that when he entered their synagogue he saw them all covering their heads with white prayer shawls (*ṭaylasān*). The kadi banned this since "this is the Muslim headgear" and they may not dress in anything that might resemble Muslim garments.

398 (b) 22 Jumādā'l-Awwal, 957: The Jews claimed they had a permit to wear this headgear, and were given a delay of 15 days to bring the permit from Damascus. In the meantime they may not wear it.

406 (a) 25 Jumādā'l-'Ūlā, 957: The heads of the Jewish community (Mūsā, Sulaymān, Yūsif, Dā'ūd, and Yūsif b. Hilāl) produced *ḥujja* and *fatwā* religious documents authorizing them to cover their heads in their synagogue with white prayer shawls (*ṭaylasān*). The kadi accepted their claim and permitted them to bring additional documents to prove their case.

460 (e) 7 Jumādā'l-Thānī, 957: A Muslim from Bayt Iksā village complained of Jews sojourning in the tomb (*maqām*) of *al-sayyid* Shmūʾīl without paying any attention to their pack animals and belongings.

535 (c) 19 Rajab, 957: Ya'qūb Falāq, the head of the Jewish community, pledged himself and his entire community to refrain from burial of any deceased Jew without a specific permit issued by the kadi.

554 (b) 26 Rajab, 957: A Muslim from Bayt Ṣafāfā village accused the Jew Ibrāhīm b. Isḥāq of owing him for 71 *raṭls* of yogurt (*laban*) he had sold him.

599 (c) 15 Sha'bān, 957: A Muslim customer complained that a shoe purchased from Yūsif b. 'Abd al-Karīm, a Jewish tanner, proved defective. The Jew was found guilty and punished.

609 (a) The middle third of Sha'bān, 957: Yūsif b. Shū'a, the Jewish tax collector (*'āmil*) in the district of Jerusalem,

acknowledged his debt of 400 *sulṭānī* gold coins to the Muslim official (*amīn*) in charge of the treasury revenues in the same district.

610 (b) The middle third of Sha'bān, 957: The poll tax for 90 Jewish people for the year 957 was paid by Ya'qūb Falāq, the head of the Jewish community, to a janissary from the Jerusalem garrison.

621 (b) End of Sha'bān, 957: Isḥāq b. Mināḥīm pledged to pay 500 *'uthmānī* to The Dome of the Rock if he sold wheat in town outside "the lot of the grains" (*'arṣat al-ghilāl*).

Volume 24
(1550 - 1551)

28 [No date provided, copied in Ramaḍān, 957.] A firman from Istanbul, a legal opinion (*fatwā*) of *shaykh al-Islām*, various testimonies of the cavalry officers (*sipāhīs*) in charge of Silwān village–a detailed description of the conflict concerning the Jewish cemetery near the Temple Mount.

39 (c) 10 Ramaḍān, 957: The kadi sold the Rabbanite Jew Sulaymān b. Aṣlān 1.25 *qinṭār* of soap for 3,900 *ḥalabiyya* to be paid in stages. Before settling his entire debt, Sulaymān left town on an alleged pilgrimage to Hebron without leaving a guarantor for the debt.

53 (c) 17 Ramaḍān, 957: The Jew Ibrāhīm b. Hilāl accused the Jew Jaḥsh b. Salāma of an attempt to stab him with a Nabulsi knife. The defendant denied the charge but on the testimony of two Jewish witnesses was convicted and flogged.

55 (b) 18 Ramaḍān, 957: The *'ifranjī* Jew Yahūdā b. Ibrāhīm b. Rūz rented a house in the Jewish quarter for 11 years for the total sum of 1,115 *ḥalabiyya* from Yahūdā b. Mūsā the Jewish money changer.

56 (a) 18 Ramaḍān, 957: The comptroller (*nāẓir*) of the endowment of *al-ribāṭ al-ḥamawī* in Jerusalem leased to the *'ifranjī* Jew Yahūdā b. Ibrāhīm b. Rūz a house in the Jewish quarter for 30 years for the total sum of 1,927 *'uthmānī*. The tenant will be exempted from all expenses incurred for the repair of this house.

120 (c) 13 Shawwāl, 957: *khōja* Yūsif b. Shū'a, the Jewish tax collector (*'āmil*) acknowledged receipt of 66 gold coins from a Nabulsi Jew who had borrowed them.

120 (d) 13 Shawwāl, 957: The above-mentioned Yūsif b. Shū'a, acknowledged that he was not entitled to any payment

or debt from the Jewish scribe for the imperial domains in Jerusalem, Yūsif b. Ibrāhīm.

182 (e) 11 Dhū'l-Qa'da, 957: Salamūn b. Mūsā Shulāl, Salamūn b. Sūkhān, Ibrāhīm *al-sayrajānī*, and Isḥāq b. Hārūn declared in court that they agreed that Yahūdā b. 'Ayzar and Ya'qūb b. Mūsā slaughter for the Jewish community on Thursdays and Mondays.

199 (c) 23 Dhū'l-Qa'da, 957: A Jew requested the court's permission to marry the widow of Ibrāhīm the Jewish tax farmer (*amīn*). The Jewish *dayyān* testified that he had already given her in marriage to another Jew who paid her bride price (6 out of a total of 11 gold coins) as well as the marriage tax. Upon testimony of a Jewish tailor and a Jewish silversmith, the court refused permission.

325 (a) 11 Ṣafar, 958: Two Muslim witnesses testify that the Jewish pearl stringer (*'aqqād*), Shmu'īl b. Dā'ūd had paid his debt of 60 gold coins to the Jewish silversmith Ya'qūb b. Yūsif, in accordance with a mediation (*ṣulḥ*) ruling reached last year. He paid in kind–43 *dhirā'* of red broad cloth (*jawkh 'arīḍ*).

325 (b) 11 Ṣafar, 958: The Jew Isḥāq b. Nātān alias al-Shanawī sold his house in the Jewish quarter (detailed description) for 25 gold coins to the Jew Ya'qūb b. Dā'ūd alias *al-ḥāmī*.

384 (c) 21 Rabī' al-Awwal, 958: A Jewish woman known as b. al-Rubayṣa *al-kaḥḥālā* sold the Rabbanite Jew Ibrāhīm b. Yūsif for the sum of 8.5 gold coins a dilapidated house she inherited in the Jewish quarter.

445 (f) 22 Rabī' al-Thānī, 958: The Jewish woman Saniyya the dressmaker (*al-khayyāṭa*) was accused by two Muslims of having received 10 *dhirā'* of blue cloth to be sewn. When she denied it they produced two Muslim witnesses who confirmed their claim.

465 (a-f) 27 Rabī' al-Thānī, 958: 5 Jewish men and 6 Jewish women admitted having climbed on a roof of the religious college building (*al-madrasa al-*

'uthmāniyya)[60] overlooking al-Aqṣā Mosque in broad daylight and emitting wine odors. They claimed to have been granted permission to do it by a Muslim dignitary who denied it categorically. All the men were condemned and flogged.

[60] For a detailed description of this religious college, see Burgoyne, pp. 544-554.

Volume 25
(1551 - 1552)

1 (a) 15 Dhū'l-Qa'da, 958: An entry in the long price list of commodities: The *muḥtasib* will inspect the bathhouses and will see to it that they be kept clean, and that a distinction be made between towels for Muslims and towels for Jews and Christians (*dhimm*). If the bathhouse operators refuse they will be flogged and pay a fine.

15 (b) 22 Shawwāl, 958: The *ṣūbāshī* of Jerusalem accused Ya'qūb Falāq, the head of the Jewish community, of having embezzled the marriage tax (*rasm al-nikāḥ*)[61] he had received from the Jew Shmū'īl instead of handing it over to him. The defendant alleged that this was Shmū'īl's poll tax . Two Jewish witnesses, Abū Ghādūr b. Ya'qūb and Bārūkh b. Yahūdā, testified that the defendant indeed received one gold coin as marriage tax.

27 (e) 3 Rajab, 958: The Jews Yahūdā b. Mūsā and Mūsā b. Salīmūn, members of the Ashkenazi (*al-aman*) Jewish community, declared that the Jew Sulaymān b. Aṣlān would be their representative spokesman (*mutakallim*) for the Ashkenazi (*al-aman*) community, according to their customs and like his predecessors in the same position.

27 (f) 3 Rajab, 958: Ya'qūb Falāq and Sulaymān b. Aṣlān, the two Jewish heads (*shaykh*) of the Jews of Jerusalem, agreed that the former would neither represent nor undertake any business of the Ashkenazi community, or collect money or spend it, and the latter would not represent the rest i.e. the non-Ashkenazi Jews who live in Jerusalem.

---

[61] Also called *resm-i arus*. Cf. Heyd, *Criminal Law*, p. 13; *EI*, s.v. "Nikāḥ."

115 (c) 13 Dhū'l-Qa'da, 958: The chief nightwatchman (*'ases bāshī*),[62] representing the *ṣūbāshī* of Jerusalem acknowledged receipt of 33 gold coins from Falāq, the head of the Jewish community, for a debt he owed the *ṣūbāshī* on account of the payment of the poll tax (*kharāj*).

127 (a) 16 Rabī' al-Thānī, 958: Tāj al-Dīn al-Sukkarī accused Falāq, the head of the Jewish community, and Mūsā b. Shulāl of not having paid their annual rent for a house he owned in equal partnership with Mināḥīm near the two bakeries in the Jewish quarter. When he had been in charge of *bayt al-māl* he gained possession of this house, he claimed, through the deceased Jew Isḥāq, then they paid him the rent.

186 (d) 22 Dhū'l-Ḥijja, 958: The Jews Yūsif b. Yahūdā, Sulaymān b. Isḥāq, Yahūdā b. Ibrāhīm, and Mūsā b. Sulaymān complained that Falāq the Jew threatened to commit suicide thereby exposing them to a great danger they might find no way of avoiding, nor will they be able to pay the fine (*jarīma*)[63] imposed on them. The court absolved them from this potential development since Falāq had been fired from his position as head of the community.

190 (d) 25 Dhū'l-Ḥijja, 958: The Jew Shiḥāda b. Abū Sa'd accused Falāq b. Ḥayyim of having collected one gold coin as marriage tax (*rasm al-nikāḥ*) from him to be given to the *ṣūbāshī*. When the defendant denied it, it was confirmed by two Jewish witnesses, Khalīfa b. Hārūn, the Damascene silversmith, and Shmū'īl b. Yūsif.

191 (c) 25 Dhū'l-Ḥijja, 958: The Jew Yūsif died outside of Jerusalem without any heirs except for his wife Rifqa. He left various belongings and a house. The official in charge of *bayt al-māl* agreed with Rifqa that she compensate him for his share by the payment of 7 gold coins.

---

[62] *EI*^{2}, s.v. "'Asas."

[63] *EI*^{2}, s.v. "Djarīma", "Djurm."

191 (d) 25 Dhū'l-Ḥijja, 958: Falāq b. Ḥayyim sold several pieces of silver jewelry (detailed list provided) to a silversmith for the sum of 15 gold coins. The jeweler declared himself willing to allow Falāq to buy back the above items within three months.

191 (e) 25 Dhū'l-Ḥijja, 958: The Jews Yūsif b. Ya'qūb *al-dayyān*, Hārūn b. 'Uriyāl, Sulaymān b. Isḥāq, and Ibrāhīm b. Ya'qūb told the court of Falāq b. Ḥayyim's intention to leave town and claim he had been expelled by them and the rest of their community. Thereupon Falāq was asked to state his case to the court and declare that if he stayed in town or left it would be of his own free will.

194 (a) 26 Dhū'l-Ḥijja, 958: When Yūsif b. Dā'ūd the Maltese Jew died he left no heirs other than his Ashkenazi Jewish wife Rifqa b. 'Ayzar. Among other things he left a two-story house he owned in the al-Rīsha quarter. His wife is entitled to one-quarter[64] and *bayt al-māl* is entitled to three-quarters of it hence the person in charge of *bayt al-māl* took possession of his share.

197 (d) 1 Muḥarram, 959: The Jew Hārūn b. Ilyār purchased from Falāq's wife, the Jewess Maryam b. Murdukhān a room she owned in a house in the Jewish quarter for 15 gold coins. She was represented in court by her husband's son, Shmū'īl.

197 (e) 1 Muḥarram, 959: The above-mentioned Hārūn purchased a bakery and half a house in the Jewish quarter from Ya'qūb Falāq, (represented by his son Shmū'īl) for the sum of 15 (?) gold coins.

198 (a) 1 Muḥarram, 959: Ya'qūb Falāq and his son Shmū'īl pledged to leave Jerusalem by the middle of the month (Shmū'īl by the end of the month) to go to Cairo and live there. If they do not go there or stay in Gaza, they will pay a fine of 100 gold coins each to the endowment of The Dome of the Rock.

---

[64] For further details, see J. Schacht, *An Introduction to Islamic Law* (Oxford, 1964), pp.169-174; J. Esposito, *Women in Muslim Family Law* (Syracuse, 1982), pp. 39-46; M. Khadduri and H. J. Liebesny, eds., *Law in the Middle East* (Washington, 1955), pp. 160-178.

198 (g) 3 Muḥarram, 959: The Jew Hārūn b. Ilyār rented a court (*ḥawsh*) in the Jewish quarter, just south of the slaughterhouse, from Ya'qūb Falāq for 100 years for the sum of 11 gold coins.

273 (b) 29 Ṣafar, 959: A group of Muslims complained that Jews were slaughtering every day and introducing their meat to the market in order to have it sold to Muslim customers, whereas in the past they used to slaughter only Mondays and Thursdays. The head of the Jewish community and the slaughterer issued documented decrees authorizing them to slaughter Mondays and Thursdays, and the kadi confirmed it.

273 (c) 29 Ṣafar, 959: Ya'qūb, the Jewish slaughterer admitted having slaughtered sheep on Wednesday and selling it to Muslim customers. He was pronounced guilty.

276 (b) End of Ṣafar, 959: (Identical with the above, on Jewish slaughtering, only) the kadi ruled that the Jews may slaughter two days a week, Mondays and Thursdays, but when there is no shortage of meat they may do so daily.

285 (a) 6 Rabī' al-Awwal, 959: The *ṣūbāshī* in his capacity as responsible for *bayt al-māl,* accompanied by the two Jewish heads of the community (Ibrāhīm b. Ya'qūb and Yūsif b. Yahūdā) went to inspect the belongings of a deceased Jewish woman. When they completed their assignment and went away the *ṣūbāshī* was told that the deceased had additional properties, kept in another house. The Jewish *shaykhs* denied it, but had to admit it when they were forced to go there again with him.

285 (e) 7 Rabī' al-Awwal, 959: Dā'ūd b. Ḥayyim the Jew admitted selling wheat to a Muslim for 35 *ḥalabiyya* per *mudd.* This was 5 more than the official price.

287 (b) 7 Rabī' al-Awwal, 959: The former chief tax collector (*amīn*) for the Imperial Domains in the Jerusalem district sued Yūsif, the son of the former Jewish clerk for the Imperial Domains, Ibrāhīm alias Tarāna, as guarantor for his father's pledge for the imperial taxes, as per a document issued by the kadi of Gaza. The

defendant claimed to have been proxy (*wakīl*) rather than guarantor (*kafīl*), but upon perusal of the document it emerged that he was to "answer" for his father, hence he was incarcerated in the Citadel of Jerusalem until the final accounts could be looked into in Damascus.

349 (b) 24 Rabīʿ al-Awwal, 959: Sulaymān b. Isḥāq and Ibrāhīm b. Hilāl and Isḥāq the tailor, speaking for the Jewish community, reported the death of Mūsā Zaqīlmān who went to the Jewish cemetery to dig out the rest of the corpses from the cave, when its roof collapsed. The court was asked to investigate it on the spot and confirmed the report.

360 (a) 27 Rabīʿ al-Thānī, 959: The Jews Yūsif b. Shūʿa, Isḥāq b. Mūsā ʿAbdūs, and Yūsif b. Ibrāhīm the physician, guaranteed the Jewish clerk Yūsif b. Ibrāhīm alias Tarāna for any claim by the former chief tax collector (*amīn*) on account of his father. Then the Jew Shentūf b. Yaʿqūb guaranteed the above Yūsif b. Shūʿa on the above matter.

364 (c) 29 Rabīʿ al-Thānī, 959: The tax collector for the districts of Jerusalem and Gaza acknowledged receipt of all outstanding debts, including those owed by the former Jewish tax collectors Shentūf b. Yaʿqūb and Yūsif b. Tarāna for the year 957-958.

398 (g) 15 Jumādā'l-Awwal, 959: The Jew Yaʿqūb b. Ḥasan leased a bakery in the Jewish quarter for 1 year and 7.5 months for 50 *ḥalabiyya* per month.

403 (c) 16 Jumādā'l-'Ūlā, 959: Members of the Jewish community came to court along with the two *muḥtasibs* of Jerusalem, complaining of lack of meat and difficulties in slaughtering. The *muḥtasibs* issued their permits to slaughter twice a week if there is a scarcity of meat and daily if there is enough meat in town. Since there was no scarcity of meat the kadi authorized them to slaughter every day and sell their meat to their community in their own neighborhood.

415 (c) 26 Jumādā'l-'Ūlā, 959: The Rabbanite Jewish *dayyān*, Nasīm b. Faraj, alias al-Fanfarī, bequeathed all his belongings to his 2 wives, Stīr and Sulṭāna, as well as to

their children Ibrāhīm, 'Abd-Allah, Sālūm, Maryam (these two are now in Cairo).

431 (e) 5 Jumādā'l-Thānī, 959: Muslims complained of Jewish daily slaughtering. The Jews Sulaymān, Ibrāhīm, and Isḥāq denied it, then agreed that their community slaughter only on Mondays and Thursdays.

464 (f) 23 Jumādā'l-Thānī, 959: 3 Muslim spice dealers (*'aṭṭār*) Jewish spice dealers (Shū'ī, Sulaymān b. Mūsā Shulāl, Ibrāhīm b. Hilāl) complained that the two *muḥtasibs* force them (*ṭarḥ*) to buy different commodities at an arbitrary price, although this constituted a breach of specific exemptions. The kadi formally announced that such practices be categorically stopped.

469 (a) 27 Jumādā'l-Thānī, 959: The Jew Sulaymān b. Shmū'īl acknowledged that there is no outstanding debt or obligation between himself and the Ashkenazi Jew Ibrāhīm b. Yābīn. He added that Ibrāhīm is entitled to the rent of a shop at the gate of "the lot of the grains" (*'arṣat al-ghilāl*).

502 (c) The middle third of Rajab, 959: Ya'qūb b. Ibrāhīm guaranteed the Jewish community to the *ṣūbāshī*: whenever any Jew is wanted by him, Ibrāhīm would personally see to it that he be brought in.

607 (c) 11 Ramaḍān, 959: The Jewish physician 'Abd al-Karīm b. Mūsā, in charge of the Karaite endowment, leased two houses in the Jewish quarter to the Ashkenazi Jew Ibrāhīm b. Mīr for 10 years for 1,200 *ḥalabiyya* annually.

607 (d) 11 Ramaḍān, 959: The above-mentioned Ibrāhīm spent 18 gold coins on repairs of one of the houses he had rented.

616 (f) 16 Ramaḍān, 959: The poll tax of 89 units (*khāne*) due from the Jewish community of Jerusalem for the year 959 was handed over to the official in charge of the tile repairs of The Dome of the Rock.

621 (c) 22 Rajab, 959: A house in the al-Sharaf quarter is owned by 'Abd-Allah the Jew.

653 (a) 4 Shawwāl, 959: The Jew Isḥāq complained that he had been assaulted at his own home by robbers who took away most of his belongings after they wounded him. When asked about it, the head of the al-Sharaf quarter said that the house in question is outside his neighborhood, it is in the Jewish quarter. The two nightwatchmen of the Jewish quarter claimed that they were hired to guard the synagogue and the shops, hence that house was outside their responsibility. The court's fact finding commission reported that the house was within the Jewish quarter and hence it was part of their responsibility.

699 (a) 2 Dhū'l-Qa'da, 959: The Karaite silversmith Ibrāhīm b. Faraj-Allah acknowledged receipt of 872 silver *qiṭ'a* from the Karaite money changer Ya'qūb b. Ibrāhīm for a debt of a third Karaite.

715 (a) 15 Dhū'l-Qa'da, 959: The Jewish physician Yūsif b. Ibrāhīm who had guaranteed Yūsif b. Ibrāhīm alias Tarāna was arrested pending his fetching of the above Yūsif.

730 (b) 25 Dhū'l-Qa'da, 959: Rifqa b. Mardūkh, the Jewish woman, guaranteed her husband Yūsif b. Ibrāhīm the Jewish physician, on account of his earlier guarantee to Yūsif b. Tarāna, the Jewish clerk.

Volume 26
(1553)

47 (d) 8 Shawwāl, 960: The kadi appointed Isḥāq b. Mūghān legal guardian of his brother's orphans: Sulaymān, Nūna and Amīra.

47 (e) 8 Shawwāl, 960: The above-mentioned Isḥāq contested an alleged purchase by a Muslim neighbor from Shams b. Faraj-Allah the mother of the above-mentioned orphans, of one-sixth of a house in al-Salatīn quarter, close to the Jewish quarter.

47 (f) 8 Shawwāl, 960: The above-mentioned Isḥāq sold to the brother of the above-mentioned Muslim about one-third of the above-mentioned house for 1,000 *'uthmānī.*

51 (e) 24 Shawwāl, 960: The Jew Salamūn b. Shulāl accused a Christian from Bayt Jālā of having received 2 gold coins from him for a consignment of 1 *qinṭār* of olive oil which he never delivered.

139 (b) 3 Ramaḍān, 960: A Muslim scholar (*faqīh*) was accused of having forced the girl Klārā b. Yūsif the Ashkenazi Jew, into his house that very morning. He denied it saying that on his way to the morning prayer he encountered her near his house, crying and looking for her sister's house. She entered his house while he was gone, then her mother heard about it and came to bring her home.

151 (c) 11 Ramaḍān, 960: The Jew Yūsif b. Mardūkh complained that a Muslim painter assaulted him and tore his headgear on an allegation that he had to be taken to the *ṣūbāshī.* The latter denied any knowledge of, or involvement in, this episode.

Volume 27
(1553 - 1554)

3 (b) 24 Rajab, 960: The Muslim clerk (*kātib*) in charge of registering income of the Imperial Domains (*al-khawāṣṣ al-sharīfa*) of the Nablus district acknowledged receipt of 11 *sulṭānī* gold coins and 22 silver coins from a Jewish silversmith, Mas'ūd b. Naftālī, in return for a gold object he had sold him.

42 (a) 9 Rajab, 960: The high official (*amīn*) in charge of the collection of poll tax (*jawālī*) income in Jerusalem acknowledged receipt of poll tax due from 89 Jews living there for the year 960. The tax was paid by the two heads (*shaykh*) of the community, Sulaymān and Ibrāhīm.

65 (c) 26 Rabī' al-Thānī, 960: The former chief tax collector (*amīn*) for the Imperial Domains of Jerusalem sued the Jew Yūsif b. Shū'a and Yūsif b. Ibrāhīm the physician who had guaranteed the Jewish clerk, Yūsif b. Ibrāhīm alias Tarāna (see above, *sijill* 25/360). The two guarantors were now arrested pending payment of an outstanding debt of the clerk's father in the Gaza district.

161 (a) 11 Jumādā'l-Thānī, 960: Muḥammad who had adopted Islam and is in charge of *bayt al-māl* of the Jews confirmed that the Jew Ya'qūb b. Mūsā owed *bayt al-māl* 7 gold coins as its share of the belongings of the deceased Jew Mūsā b. Ibrāhīm.

161 (b) 11 Jumādā'l-Thānī, 960: The above-mentioned Muḥammad attested to a debt of 8 gold coins owed by the Jew Isḥāq b. Hārūn to the *bayt al-māl* of the Jews for its share of the belongings of the deceased, Qādūr the Jew.

161 (c) 11 Jumādā'l-Thānī, 960: The above-mentioned Muḥammad attested to a debt of 8 gold coins owed by

the Jew Rūbīn for his share of the belongings of his deceased wife, Malīḥa.

162 (a) 11 Jumādā'l-Thānī, 960: The above-mentioned Muḥammad attested to a debt of 7 gold coins owed by the Jewess Yartīnā b. Shmū'īl on account of the share of *bayt al-māl* of the Jews from the inheritance of her deceased husband, Mūsā b. Ibrāhīm.

162 (b) 11 Jumādā'l-Thānī, 960: A list of silver utensils, silver pieces of jewelry and silver coins which had been held in custody of the above-mentioned Muḥammad, just released and returned to their owner, the Jew Rūbīn b. Mināḥim.

163 (d) 12 Jumādā'l-Thānī, 960: A list of belongings of the deceased Jew 'Akka.

163 (e) 11 Jumādā'l-Thānī, 960: The above-mentioned Muḥammad confirms receipt of all the above-mentioned debts from Rūbīn, Yartīnā, Ya'qūb and Hārūn–a total of 30 gold coins they owed *bayt al-māl* of the Jews.

188 (d) 18 Dhū'l-Qa'da, 960: The Jewish tanner Ya'qūb was sued by a Muslim whom another Jew, Yūsif b. Hilāl, owed a sum of money Ya'qūb had underwritten.

307 (d) The first third (*awā'il*) of Ṣafar, 961: The Sublime Porte, by way of answering an earlier petition sent by the Jews of Jerusalem, issued a decree prohibiting any further attempts of forced purchase (*ṭarḥ*) of goods in Jerusalem. The kadi orders the local *muḥtasib* to refrain from similar attempts in the future.

314 (c) 13 Ṣafar, 961: The kadi upholds a complaint submitted by the Jew Isḥāq b. 'Azar that he had been sold meat at an inflated price.

336 (c) 28 Ṣafar, 961: A report issued by a special committee sent by the kadi to ascertain the exact measurements of a reconstructed house built by the Jew Ibrāhīm b. Hilāl. Special attention is paid to avoid infringing on any private or public rights.

Volume 28
(1554)

45 (c) [No date mentioned.] Zubayda b. Ḥānān, the Jewish legal guardian of her three orphans, sold to the Jew Ibrāhīm b. Isḥāq b. Sabatūn various silversmith's utensils for 2 gold coins.

139 (a) 2 Muḥarram, 962: The Jewess Qamar b. Ya'qūb sold 2 rooms in a house she inherited in the Jewish quarter to a Muslim. The price paid was 10 gold coins. It was agreed that this sale be regarded as a temporary one (*bay' bi'l-wafā'*).

169 (b) 18 Ramaḍān, 961: The Jew Ya'qūb b. Yūsif confirmed that 13 years earlier he had granted possession (*tamlīk*) of two rooms in his house in al-Rīsha quarter to his daughter Qamar, Murdakhay's wife.

220 (a) 16 Shawwāl, 961: Two imperial decrees were sent to Jerusalem forbidding any attempt to stop Jewish pilgrims from visiting (*ziyāra*) the tomb of the prophet Shmū'īl.

222 (b) 10 Rabī' al-Thānī, 961: A very detailed description of a sale of certain parts of a house in Jerusalem owned by the Jew Isḥāq b. Mināḥim Qāṭān, to a Jew from Cairo, for the sum of 70 gold coins.

251 (a) 5 Jumādā'l-'Ūlā, 961: The Jew 'Abd al-Qādir b. Ya'īsh owes a Muslim 14 gold coins; his son guarantees this debt.

251 (c) 6 Jumādā'l-'Ūlā, 961: The road tax (*khafar*) levied on Jewish pilgrims to the tomb of the prophet Shmū'īl was leased out to two Muslims who raised their price by 200 percent for the period of the 2 months of Jumādā of this year.

258 (d) 12 Jumādā'l-'Ūlā, 961: The Jew Yahūdā b. Ya'qūb, the slaughterer (*dhabbāḥ*) of the Jewish community, vows

to slaughter only on Mondays and Thursdays and to refrain from introducing his meat into the general market.

260 (c) 13 Jumādā'l-'Ūlā, 961: The Jew Yahūdā al-Faranjī ("the European" i.e. Ashkenazi) was found guilty of selling unleavened bread (*kmāj*) using faulty weights: one *raṭl* was missing one *'uqiyya*.

310 (a) 10 Jumādā'l-Thānī, 961: The Jew Isḥāq b. Isra'īl b. Yaḥya claimed that the Jewess Shahīda b. Ḥānān owed him 10 gold coins she had borrowed from him and mortgaged half of her house in al-Rīsha quarter (neighboring buildings, including a soap factory, are mentioned).

310 (b) 12 Jumādā'l-Thānī, 961: The above-mentioned property (a detailed description provided) was sold to the above-mentioned *al-mu'allim* Isḥāq for 70 gold coins.

311 (d) 12 Jumādā'l-Thānī, 961: The four sons of the above-mentioned Shahīda declare her full ownership rights to the above-mentioned property.

316 (b) 16 Jumādā'l-Thānī, 961: Seven Jewish ladies (names provided) admitted having climbed to the roof of the religious college building (*al-madrasa al-manjakiyya*)[65] overlooking the Temple Mount in order to look at al-Aqṣā Mosque.

317 (a) 15 Jumādā'l-Thānī, 961: The Jew Falāq purchased a storage room and a bakery located south of the slaughtering house from the Jew Hārūn b. Ilyār for the sum of 15 gold coins.

317 (b) 15 Jumādā'l-Thānī, 961: The Jewess Maryam b. Murdukhān, the wife of Ya'qūb Falāq, purchased a house from Hārūn b. Ilyār for the sum of 15 gold coins.

317 (c) 15 Jumādā'l-Thānī, 961: The above-mentioned Ya'qūb mortgaged the above-mentioned bakery to the above-mentioned Hārūn against his debt of 16 gold coins.

---

[65] For a detailed description, see Burgoyne, pp. 384-398.

317 (e) 17 Jumādā'l-Thānī, 961: The Jew Ya'qūb b. Ibrāhīm b. Isḥāq paid his debt to an Egyptian Muslim.

318 (c) 17 Jumādā'l-Thānī, 961: A very detailed inventory of all the belongings of the deceased Jew Salamūn b. Isḥāq inherited by his wife Astār b. Salamūn.

323 (c) 21 Jumādā'l-Thānī, 961: The Jew Hārūn b. Ilyār brought to the court a black female slave. She claimed to have been in the service of a Jewish person who left Jerusalem and deserted her outside the town, whereupon she was put under custody of the officer in charge of runaway slaves.

333 (a) 27 Jumādā'l-Thānī, 961: The Jewess Stīr b. Ibrāhīm the widow of Hārūn the blind Jew was granted a court order attesting to her ownership of two houses in the Jewish quarter close to the old town gate.

333 (c) 29 Jumādā'l-Thānī, 961: The two above-mentioned houses were endowed (*waqf)* by the above-mentioned woman.

383 (d) 24 Rajab, 961: The Jew Yūsif b. Ibrāhīm alias *al-sayrajānī* ("the sesame oil dealer") guaranteed the Jew Aṣlān b. Mūsā in a dispute over grapes.

445 (a) 10 Ramaḍān, 961: A Muslim and the Jew Ya'qūb b. Ḥasan declare that there is no legal dispute or outstanding obligation between them.

447 (a) 2 Ramaḍān, 961: The Jewess Samiyya b. Ibrāhīm purchased from the Jew 'Ubayd b. Ya'īsh half of a house in the Jewish quarter for the sum of 550 silver coins (*dirham*).

Volume 29
(1517 - 1555)

13[66] The last third (*awākhir*) of Rabīʿ al-Ākhir, 956: A Sultanic decree issued in Aleppo and addressed to the kadi of Jerusalem. The Jewish community of Jerusalem sent a petition to the Sultan describing a variety of acts of harassment perpetrated by the local authorities: whenever they (the Jews) wanted to have a sheep slaughtered or a house built, although the item involved was in their own possession, they were forced to pay a special fine. If their allegation proved to be valid, this harassment should be immediately discontinued.

29[67] The second third (*awāsiṭ*) of Jumādā'l Awwal, 961: A Sultanic decree issued in Aleppo and based on a petition sent by the Jewish communities in Damascus and Palestine. When they go on pilgrimage to Jerusalem and Hebron they are not allowed to enter these towns unless they pay an unlawful exorbitant fine. If this proves to be the case, the district governor and the kadi should stop all such levies.

72[68] (a) The first third (*awā'il*) of Jumādā'l Awwal, 961: A Sultanic decree issued in Aleppo and addressed to the kadi of Jerusalem. A petition sent by the Jewish community of Jerusalem described a pattern of unlawful behavior in Jerusalem. The owners of a plot of land used by the Jews as their cemetery from time immemorial threaten to lease it to others and dig out the remains of their people buried therein. The decree orders that an inquiry into the matter be conducted, and if this is substantiated it should be stopped.

73[69] (a) The second third (*awāsiṭ*) of Rabīʿ al-Ākhir, 961: A Sultanic decree sent from Aleppo to the governor and

---

[66] Turkish.
[67] Turkish.
[68] Turkish.
[69] Turkish.

the kadi of Jerusalem, based on a petition submitted in Istanbul. The local authorities (*muḥtasib, ṣūbāshī*) in Jerusalem permit the slaughtering of animals by the Jews only twice a week, pending payment of a special fine. Any linkage of this kind should be discontinued, they should be permitted to slaughter any time, and the forced purchase of sheep at exorbitant prices should not be authorized.

73[70] (b) The second third (*awāsiṭ*) of Jumādā'l-Awwal, 961: A Sultanic decree sent from Aleppo to the governor and kadi of Jerusalem, based on a petition submitted in Istanbul. Jews who come as pilgrims to Jerusalem, then return to their original homes are still being referred to as local inhabitants, hence liable to poll tax . Since they are liable for this tax in their permanent places of abode, this policy should be discontinued.

73[71] (c) A legal opinion (*fatwā*) according to the Hanafite school on the question of whether Muslims may eat meat that was slaughtered by Jews. The answer is: yes, it is permissible.

79[72] (a) The second third (*awāsiṭ*) of Rabī‘ al-Ākhir, 961: A Sultanic decree addressed to the judge and the governor of Jerusalem, based on a petition submitted in Istanbul. The local authorities penalize the Jews living in Jerusalem and harass them when they cover their heads with a white (rather than the authorized yellow) shawl in their synagogues. If this claim is validated, it should be discontinued.

122[73] The last third (*awākhir*) of Rabī‘ al-Ākhir, 923: The Rabbanite Jewish community submitted a petition to the Sultan describing how the Karaite Jews stopped them from visiting (*ziyāra*) the site named after Shmū'il of Ramā village. The Sultan decreed that were this found to be true, it should be discontinued.

---

[70] Turkish.
[71] Turkish.
[72] Turkish.
[73] Turkish.

167[74] The first third (*awā'il*) of Muḥarram, 963: A Sultanic decree addressed to the governor and the kadi of Jerusalem, based on a petition submitted in Istanbul by the Jewish community living in Jerusalem. They reported that Jewish pilgrims used to visit an old synagogue that belonged to them and was called Sayyid Shmū'il. It was turned into a mosque, hence they could no longer visit it. The Sultan decreed that if their allegation was substantiated this harassment of the Jews should be discontinued.

[74] Turkish.

Volume 30

(1555)

238 (b) Sha'bān, 962: A group of jewelers came to court, including a few Christians and the Jews: Mas'ūd b. Ibrāhīm, the Karaite Ibrāhīm b. Faraj Allah, Da'ūd b. 'Amrān and Ibrāhīm b. Isḥāq. They complained that the two inspectors of the markets (*muḥtasib*) of town kept interfering in their business and checking their weights. They do so in spite of the fact that an explicit order as well as old custom warn against such behavior. When the kadi saw the old document he summoned the *muḥtasibs* and warned them against any further interference.

248 (d) 27 Sha'bān, 962: A kadi of Hebron who is the administrator (*mutawallī*) of the charitable endowment of Tamīm al-Dārī in that town accused Isḥāq, the head of the Jewish community of Jerusalem, of not complying with their obligation to provide this endowment with the annual sum of 50 silver coins. When Isḥāq admitted guilt and the relevant document was consulted the kadi ruled that the above sum should be paid.

268 (d) 10 Ramaḍān, 962: A Muslim absolves Isḥāq b. Ibrāhīm, Yūsif *al-dayyān* ("the rabbi") and all other members of the Jewish community of any outstanding debt, and most specifically of the sum of 25 gold coins they owed him.

390 (e) 12 Dhū'l-Qa'da, 962: The scribe for the Imperial Domains revenue (*al-khawāṣṣ al-sharīfa*) in the district of Nablus claimed that the Jewish jeweler Mas'ūd b. Naftālī owed him 20 gold coins (the official rate of which is 40 Sulaymānī silver coins each) for a consignment of 10 loads (*ḥiml*)of wheat (each load measuring 16 Jerusalemite *mudd*) he had bought from him 16 months earlier. The plaintiff could not provide any proof of his claim whereas the defendant swore that

he owed him nothing. Thereupon the court was adjourned.

Volume 31
(1556)

117 (a) 22 Rabī' al-Awwal, 963: Muḥammad Bey, a *sipāhī* from Lajjūn,was commissioned with the collection of taxes due from the District of Damascus. He formally acknowledged receipt of the poll tax due from the Jewish community of Jerusalem for the year 963 A.H. Salamūn b. Mūsā Shulāl and Yāsif b. 'Abd al-Karīm, in charge of the Jewish community (*mutakallim),* confirmed that the 89 tickets they paid represented the exact number of members of the community.

126 (a) 26 Rabī' al-Awwal, 963: Heads of various communities confirm payment of all poll tax dues for the year 963 A.H. For the Jewish community, Salamūn b. Mūsā Shulāl, Yāsif b. 'Abd al-Karīm, Ibrāhīm b. Hilāl and Isḥāq the Jew are referred to as responsible spokesmen (*mutakallim*).

181 (c) The last third (*awākhir*) of Rabī' al-Thānī, 963: The Jew Shū'a b. Nassīm guaranteed the Jew Yūsif b. Ḥayyim "as is the case with the inhabitants of the neighborhoods (*maḥalla)*" that if the *ṣūbāshī* request his presence and he does not oblige, Shū'a will be held personally responsible according to the *sharī'a* and the *qānūn.*[75]

181 (d-f) The last third (*awākhir*) of Rabī' al-Thānī, 963: Identical guarantees (*kafāla)* by other Jews for their coreligionists.

187 (d) First of Jumādā'l-Awwal, 963: The Jew Shmū'āl b. Abū Jūkār was indicted for selling meat to a Muslim at an inflated price. He was duly condemned and punished.

188 (j) First of Jumādā'l-Awwal, 963: A Muslim merchant sued the Jew Khalīfa b. Yakīlmān for a debt of 5 gold

[75] On these two terms, see Heyd, *Criminal Law,* pp. 174, 180-183, 186-192.

coins. The defendant admitted guilt and was duly condemned.

250 (d) 13 Jumādā'l-Awwal, 963: A group of Muslims came to the Shāfi'ī kadi complaining of the Jewish slaughtering and requesting that it be banned to Muslim customers. The Jewish slaughterer Ya'qūb b. Mūsā, as well as the Jews Yamṭūn b. Mas'ūd and Shmū'īl b. Abū Jūkār were summoned to the court and explicitly warned that they should stamp the slaughtered meat "according to their custom" and sell it in their neighborhood only.

251 (e) 13 Jumādā'l-Awwal, 963: A Muslim butcher vowed in front of the Shāfi'ī kadi to refrain from any slaughtering for the Jews or in the Jewish manner that would be sold later to Muslim customers in the marketplace.

303 (d) 13 Jumādā'l-Thānī, 963: The *ṣūbāshī* of Jerusalem accused the Jewish cloth merchant (*jawkhī*)[76] of contravening a formal oath (*qasama*) forbidding any Jew from entering the Holy Sepulcher or even passing by its gate. The defendant, 'Āzir b. Ibrāhīm, admitted that he had entered the place in his capacity as a translator to the Catholic pilgrims who arrived there and that he had no former knowledge of the above-mentioned warning. The kadi summoned several highly placed Muslim officials who supported the case of the Jew. Hence he was acquitted.

304 (a) 16 Jumādā'l-Thānī, 963: The Jew Shmū'īl b. Jūkār vowed to refrain from selling cheese outside Jerusalem.

305 (h) 16 Jumādā'l-Thānī, 963: An Exalted order arrived from Istanbul forbidding the Jewish community from going into the tomb (*maqām*) of Shmū'īl outside Jerusalem. The district governor and the kadi summoned the heads of the community and accordingly prohibited them from entering the place.

320 (c) 25 Jumādā'l-Thānī, 963: The Jew Yūsif b. Jalkhīn authorized a Muslim from the village of Shafā 'Amr to sell half of a house that he owned in Jerusalem.

---

[76] For the origins of this term , see *Population and Revenue*, p. 60, n. 43.

320 (g) 24 Jumādā'l-Thānī, 963: As of the beginning of the year 951 the Jew Yūsif b. Jalkhīn b. Dawīd had leased half of his house in the Jewish quarter (*ḥārat al-yahūd*) to the Jew Mināḥīm b. Ma'tūq for a twenty year period and for the total sum of 1,000 silver coins.

380 (b) 22 Rajab, 963: The Damascene Jew Mūsā b. Shmū'īl bought from the building authorities 1,200 *qinṭār* of lead waste that accumulated as a result of repairs conducted on the roof of al-Aqṣā Mosque.

432 (e) 22 Sha'bān, 963: The Jews Sulaymān b. Dā'ūd and his mother accuse a Jewish jeweler, Mas'ūd b. al-Fatārī, in conjunction with the disappearance of their brother and son while he was travelling on business to Qabāṭiyyā.

435 (f) 20 Sha'bān, 963: Many Jerusalemites complained to the kadi about the scarcity of meat and its actual disappearance from the city markets. Thereupon eight butchers were brought to the court, one of whom was the Jew Shmū'īl b. Abū Jūkār. They all vowed to provide the city with sufficient quantities of meat to last until the end of Ramaḍān. They also pledged not to leave Jerusalem without the specific permission of the kadi. (For a similar and more detailed list of butchers, including the same Jew, see page 452 (c)).

436 (c) 24 Sha'bān, 963: The Jew Mas'ūd b. al-Naftārī was once again accused of the death of the Jew Mas'ūd b. Dā'ūd in Nablus. He took an oath "in accordance with his [religious] principle" that he had no link to the alleged killing and was thereupon exonerated.

450 (a) 1 Ramaḍān, 963: A group of Jews including Suwaydān b. Ibrāhīm, Dā'ūd b. Mūkhāy, Raḥamīm b. Yūsif, Shamīla b. Falāq, Ramīn b. 'Awaḍ–came to the court. In spite of the valid official order that they not be molested they have been exposed to a variety of acts of harassment brought about by the Muslim head of the al-Rīsha quarter. Since the latter could not offer any lawful reason for his behavior, he was removed from his official position and replaced as head of the Jewish quarter (*ḥārat al-yahūd)* by another Muslim whom the Jews recommended.

533 (d) 11 Shawwāl, 963: The Jew Shamīla b. Abū Jūkār sued a Muslim from Ṣūr Bāhir for the amount of 2 gold coins for the sale of a consignment of watermelons.

534 (e) 12 Shawwāl, 963: Two Jewish women, Mallāḥ b. Dā'ūd and Stayta b. Sulaymān, were fined by the court for their physical and verbal fight.

550 (c) 20 Shawwāl, 963: A Jewish jeweler, Ibrāhīm b. Faraj-Allah, locked his shop at the end of the day and returned home from the market (*sūq al-tujjār*). The next morning, when he came to open it he found to his dismay that it had been broken into and a variety of silver pieces (weights and terms provided) had been stolen.

554 (c) 24 Shawwāl, 963: Shamīla b. Jūkār, the head of the Jewish community (*shaykh al-yahūd*) was accused of mishandling a plot of land leased to him outside the Jewish quarter by allowing members of his community to dispose of their garbage therein. When his denial was refuted by a fact-finding committee he claimed that the place had been rented out by the plaintiff to another Jew. The court granted him a three day delay to submit the written proof he claimed was available.

560 (e) 8 Shawwāl, 963: A Muslim sued the Jew Yūsif b. 'Abd al-Karīm for the rest of his salary as a guard of the latter's neighborhood. The defendant admitted that he had hired his (the Muslim's) services for which he had paid him all that was his due.

591 (h) 19 Dhū'l-Qa'da, 963: The Jew Ya'qūb Falāq owed a Muslim merchant the sum of 4,500 silver coins in return for 90 *raṭl* of soap that he sold and delivered to him. Ya'qūb mortgaged a cellar, a bakery and a room in a house (detailed locations provided) by way of guaranteeing his debt.

599 (b) 23 Dhū'l-Qa'da, 963: The Jew Shmū'īl b. Ya'qūb Falāq bought a consignment of soap from a Muslim. He was granted a delay of one year to actually pay the sum of 3760 silver coins that he owed in return for the 62 *raṭl* and 11 *'uqiyya* of soap. His father came to the court and guaranteed (*kafāla*) the debt of his son.

Volume 32
(1554 - 1556)

7[77] The second third (*awāsiṭ*) of Jumādā'l-Awwal, 961: A Sultanic decree sent from Aleppo was based on a petition submitted by the Jewish community of Jerusalem. The local authorities, based on false accusations that the Jews of Jerusalem cursed Islam, forced them to wear a bell when they entered the public bath, forced their women to wear yellow, and threatened to disinter the remains of their dead. The Sultan decreed that if this report proved to be true this pattern of behavior should be discontinued.

11[78] (a) The second third (*awāsiṭ*) of Rabī' al-Ākhir, 961: A Sultanic decree sent from Aleppo to the governor and the kadi of Jerusalem, based on a petition submitted by the Jews living in Jerusalem. Attempts were made by Muslims in Jerusalem to rob them of houses they legally owned by fabricating false accusations and even producing false evidence. If such reports proved to be true, this treacherous behavior should be discontinued.

164[79] (a) The first third (*awā'il*) of Jumādā'l-Ākhir, 963: A Sultanic decree addressed to the governor and the kadi of Jerusalem, based on a petition submitted by the Jews living in Jerusalem and its vicinity. The officials charged with the collection of their poll tax levy higher sums than prescribed by the *sharī'a* or actually authorized by the tax registers. They include in their lists missing or even dead people, they add baseless levies under a variety of terms (*kesr-i mīzān*, *ṣarrāfliq*, *rej' aqchesī*), and they fail to provide proper receipts. The Sultan decreed that if these allegations are validated all these patterns of behavior should be discontinued.

---

[77] Turkish.
[78] Turkish.
[79] Turkish.

167[80] The last third (*awākhir*) of Rajab, 963: A Sultanic decree addressed to the governor and kadi of Jerusalem, based on a petition submitted by the Jews of Jerusalem. The local officials in charge of *bayt al-māl* harass them by the unsolicited application to them of Muslim laws of inheritance or by disregarding valid evidence submitted by the actual heirs. The Sultan decreed that all such behavior should be discontinued.

168-169[81] The last third (*awākhir*) of Jumādā'l-Ākhir, 963: A Sultanic decree addressed to the governors and the kadis of the province of Damascus, based on Jewish petitions submitted to the Sultan. They reported unlawful impositions on the Jewish communities: military units are accomodated in their houses, they are taken to compulsory labor on days they regard as holy, forced conversion to Islam is practiced on their children, etc. This decree should be copied into the court's proceedings so that future kadis, like the incumbent ones, would be able to act upon it and discontinue such acts of harassment if they occur.

[80] Turkish.
[81] Turkish.

Volume 33
(1556 - 1557)

30 (c) The first third (*awā'il*) of Muḥarram, 964: A Muslim sued the Ashkenazi (*al-amanī*) Jew Isḥāq b. Ibrahīm who allegedly molested him and cursed his parents. When no adequate proof was produced the defendant was acquitted.

71 (c) 21 Muḥarram, 964: The Jewess Sāra b. Dā'ūd (physical description provided) admitted owing 40 *sulṭānī* gold coins to the Jew Yūsif b. Ya'qūb b. Yahūdā. She had borrowed this sum from him in Alexandria so that she might set herself free from "the Catholic (*'ifranj*) community" who were holding her in captivity. She paid him 10 gold coins, then she hired herself out to his wife Sulṭāna as her personal maid for a period of ten years in return for the rest of her debt.

127 (a) 24 Ṣafar, 964: The Damascene Karaite Jew Sulaymān b. 'Abd al-'Azīz declares in court that neither the governor, his deputy, or any other member of their entourage owe him anything.

127 (b) 19 Ṣafar, 964: The Karaite Jew Ibrāhīm b. Faraj-Allah guaranteed his brother 'Abd al-Rahīm, as well as Yūsif b. Isḥāq and 'Abd al-Karīm b.'Abd al-Laṭīf–all of them Jerusalemite Karaites. This is a formal guarantee (*kafāla*) that if they fail to present themselves to the *ṣūbāshī* upon his summons then Ibrāhīm will be held personally accountable.

128 (a) 19 Ṣafar, 964: The aforementioned Ibrāhīm absolves the governor, his deputy and his *ṣūbāshī* of any financial or other obligation to him.

140 (g) 26 Ṣafar, 964: A group of jewelers, including the Jews Ibrahīm b. Faraj-Allah, Dā'ūd b. Shmū'īl and Yūsif b. Ibrahīm undertook in the presence of the *muḥtasib* to meet and practice their profession in one market only.

144 (d) 3 Rabīʿ al-Awwal, 964: After the above-mentioned agreement among the jewelers was reached, two silversmiths came to court and asked that it not be applied to them. The Jews Dāʾūd b. Shmūʾīl and Masʿūd b. al-Aftālī argued that they had rented a shop at the *sūq al-qushshāsh* market from the Shāfiʿī kadi for two years. The permission they requested was granted until their lease expires.

145 (d) 4 Rabīʿ al-Awwal, 964: The Jewish silversmith Yūsif b. Ibrāhīm requested that he be permitted to continue to use the shop he had rented from the authorities of the al-Aqṣā endowment and postpone his transfer to the jewelers' market within the Merchants' Market (*sūq al-tujjār)*. Permission was granted until his lease expires.

159 (a) The middle third (*awāsiṭ*) of Rabīʿ al-Awwal, 964: A group of Jewish wheat dealers (*ḥaddār*) (several names given) complained that they were being harassed and unjustly taxed by the local policing forces (*ṣūbāshiyya* and *ʿasasiyya)* on the false accusation that they had been buying their grains from the bedouins. Although they actually make their purchases in the villages surrounding Jerusalem they are required to pay an indemnity (*jarīma*) up to the rate of one tithe (*ʿushr*) on the grains they bring into their houses in Jerusalem. The kadi ruled that in accordance with an earlier Sultanic order (*firmān*) they had produced in court, the *ṣūbāshī* should refrain from all harassment based on such or similar allegations.

197 (b) 27 Rabīʿ al-Awwal, 964: An order was sent from the governor of Damascus to the governor of Jerusalem to look into a matter brought up by a Damascene Jew, Salamūn b.ʿAbd al-ʿAzīz. While in Jerusalem he was forced to pay–along with the staff serving in the synagogue there–an indemnity of 150 *sulṭānī* gold coins to the *ṣūbāshī*. The synagogue was also sealed on the false allegation that it was a new one (*ḥāditha)*. Moreover, the governor of Jerusalem confiscated the formal document they had at their disposal attesting to its being an old institution there.

When the above-mentioned Salamūn was summoned to court along with one of the staff of the synagogue,

Ibrāhīm b. Faraj-Allah, they replied that the old document was still at their disposal and that the governor had not molested them or fined them. However, the *ṣūbāshī* of Jerusalem had molested them and actually levied an unjustifiable fine of 135 gold coins in conjunction with the "synagogue case." The *ṣūbāshī* denied their allegation and presented an earlier official court document (*ḥujja*) in which the aforementioned Jews specifically absolved him of any debt or obligation. Thereupon the kadi admitted this document and accordingly acquitted the *ṣūbāshī*.

235 (f) 21 Rabīʻ al-Thānī, 964: The Jew Ibrāhīm b. ʻAbd-Allah requested the kadi's permission to leave town for the villages in the sub-district (*nāḥiya*) of Jerusalem in order to produce cheese for their community "in accordance with their old custom." Permission was granted.

294 (e) 24 Jumādā'l-Awwal, 964: The Jew Manḥūna b. Maʻtūq reported to the *ṣūbāshī* that three out of the four shops in the Jewish quarter leased from the Muslim religious (*waqf*) authorities had become dilapidated. The poor Jews who had occupied them left, hence he remained the only person in charge of lighting the lamp (*qindīl*) hanging on the vaulted passageway (*qanṭara*) there. His request to be absolved from this duty was granted.

365 (b) 2 Rajab, 964: The official sent from Damascus to collect the annual poll tax (*jizya*) acknowledged receipt of all the tax due from 89 people liable for the year 964 A.H. He handed over a formal receipt (*rajʻa*) to the head of the Jewish community (*shaykh al-yahūd*), Shmū'īl b. Abū Jūkār.

380 (e) 11 Rajab, 964: The head of the night watchers (*ʻases bāshī*) accused the Jew ʻĀzir b. ʻUbayd of having beaten his wife Maryam b. Mūsā until he broke her arm. The accused denied it and was upheld by the woman who stated that she fractured her arm when she fell off a mule she was riding.

406 (b) 26 Rajab, 964: The Rabbanite Jew Saʻīd b. Yaʻqūb claimed that a certain Christian person with whom he had deposited several items would not admit that they

included 6 *sulṭānī* gold coins. Unlike the other items he handed over to another Jew in Damascus as per their agreement, the Christian denied receipt of this sum altogether. Two Muslim witnesses confirmed the plaintiff's claim, and the kadi ruled in favor of the Jew.

422 (b) 8 Sha'bān, 964: A high-ranking officer guaranteed the Jew Yūsif b. Mūsā for any monetary or other claim that might be related to the governor of Jerusalem.

466 (a) 3 Ramaḍān, 964: A Muslim merchant, to whom the late Ya'qūb Falāq owed money, bought a room from his widow in one house she owned, a cellar in another (a detailed description provided), mostly against his (Falāq's) debt that was long overdue.

473 (f) 7 Ramaḍān, 964: The kadi issued a formal permit to the Jew 'Ānū b. 'Āzir to conduct marriages among members of his community, to issue the relevant documents and to collect the various taxes due from marriage contracts, legacies and any other documents he might put together.

486 (a) 15 Ramaḍān, 964: The *muḥtasib* of Jerusalem accused the Jew Shamīla b. Abū Jūkār of using false weights as well as of being five months late in paying his dues for his butcher shop.

528 (e) 21 Shawwāl, 964: The *ṣūbāshī* of Jerusalem confirmed that all land taxes due to the imperial Treasury for the year 963 A.H. were collected by the Jew Yūsif b. Mūsā as part of his lease. The total sum collected was 88 *sulṭānī* gold coins and 10 silver coins.

530 (c) 21 Shawwāl, 964: The Jew Ibrāhīm b. Hilāl upon arrival at his shop in the spice dealers' market (*sūq al-'aṭṭārīn*) discovered that one of its locks had been broken open and a variety of items was missing (details provided).

Volume 34
(1560)

91[82] The last third (*awākhir*) of Rajab, 967: A Sultanic decree addressed to the governor and the kadi of Jerusalem, based on a petition sent by the Jewish community of Jerusalem. They had been leasing from the al-Jismāniyya endowment a certain area near Jerusalem which they used as their cemetery. Recent conflicts with the administrator (*mutawallī*) of the endowment as to the annual sum they should pay for their lease, brought about a threat by the administrator that he may order a disinternment of their dead from their graves, and might discontinue the authorization to have a cemetery there. The Sultan decreed that a thorough investigation into this matter be conducted and no act of injustice or harassment be inflicted on the Jews.

[82] Turkish.

Volume 35
(1557 - 1558)

12 (c) The last third (*awākhir*) of Dhū'l-Qaʻda, 964: The head of the Jewish community (*shaykh ṭā'ifat al-yahūd*), Shmū'īl b. Jūkār, and the Jew Yūsif b. Sabtūn guaranteed the latter's brother in all monetary and other matters in case he fails to appear before the *ṣūbāshı* when summoned.

12 (f) The last third (*awākhir*) of Dhū'l-Qaʻda, 964: The Muslim dignitary in charge of the charitable endowments in Jerusalem, leased to the Karaite Jewish physician ʻAbd al-Karīm b. Mūsā three vaulted buildings and a water cistern in al-Sharaf quarter. The lease is for nine years and its total value is ninety silver coins.

38 (c) 22 Dhū'l-Ḥijja, 964: A Muslim merchant sold the Jew Shmū'īl b. Yaʻqūb Falāq a variety of spices (details provided) which the latter stocked in his shop at the spice dealers' market (*sūq al-ʻaṭṭārīn*) adjacent to that of the Jewish physician ʻAbd al-Karīm. Shmū'īl had mortgaged his shop to the Muslim who now demanded full payment. Since he could not pay his debt Shmū'īl was arrested.

38 (e) 22 Dhū'l-Ḥijja, 964: A Christian merchant sold Shmū'īl b. Yaʻqūb Falāq a variety of spices which he mortgaged pending payment of his debt. When he denied his debt a Muslim witness attested to its validity, whereupon he was condemned.

66 (b) 8 Muḥarram, 965: The Jew Isḥaq in his capacity as the person in charge (*mutakallim*) of the Jewish community applied for a permit to repair the roofs of their synagogue and the adjoining building. Upon inspection permission was granted.

85 (d) 18 Dhū'l-Qaʻda, 964: The Jews Isḥāq b. Ibrāhīm, Salamūn b. Mūsā and Shmū'īl b. Jūkār complained that

they are not allowed to buy grapes. The kadi consulted his sources, then granted them the permission they requested provided they sell no wine to the Muslims.

86 (b) 29 Shawwāl, 964: Farrūkh Bey, the former district governor, acknowledged his debt to the Jew Ya'qūb b. Alūyā at the rate of 210 gold coins in return for a consignment of cloth (type and quantity provided) he had bought from him.

128 (b) 8 Ṣafar, 965: The Jews Shmū'īl b. Ya'qūb Falāq, his sister Najma and her mother Mas'ūda b. Ḥayyim confirmed a Muslim merchant's purchase from their mother of a room and a vaulted cellar located in the Jewish quarter. They acknowledged that they had no objection to it, nor would their other sister oppose the sale.

135 (c) 15 Ṣafar, 965: A Muslim merchant acknowledged receipt of payment for the largest part of a substantial debt from Shmū'īl b. Ya'qūb Falāq, his sister, and "other spice dealers".

178 (a) 14 Rabī' al-Awwal, 965: The Jewish community sent a messenger to Istanbul to complain of the maltreatment they are exposed to in Jerusalem. When a member of their community dies the kadis do not allow them to apply their own rules of inheritance and rather compel them to act according to those of the Islamic law. Thereupon a Sultanic order was sent instructing the court to seek a legal opinion (*fatwā*) and the Jews actually presented the court with one issued by the highest authority in the Empire, Shaykh Abū'l Su'ūd Efendi, the *muftī* of Istanbul.[83] His ruling was that nothing should be done to stop them from applying their own laws. The kadi ruled therefore that as long as the Jews do not specifically ask for application of the *sharī'a* laws in the context of their inheritances they should not be stopped from applying their own.

---

[83] Shaykh Abū'l Su'ūd was the highest religious and legal authority during the days of Suleiman the Magnificent. For a selection of his legal opinions, see M. Ertuğrul Düzdağ, *Şeyhülislâm Ebussuûd Efendi Fetvaları ışığında 16 asır türk hayatı* (Istanbul, 1972).

179 (g) 15 Rabīʿ al-Awwal, 965: The comptroller (*nāẓir*) of the mosque located in the Jewish neighborhood complained that since the "wall of the shops of the Jewish endowment" fell down, dogs can get to the roof of the mosque and desecrate it. A group of experts was sent to inspect the place and they verified that the dilapidated eastern wall bordered the mosque on its southern as well as its western side. The kadi therefore instructed the Jew in charge of the Jewish charitable endowments, Yaʿqūb *al-dayyān,* to have this wall rebuilt without adding anything thereto.

Volume 36
(1558)

6 (a) 11 Jumādā'l-'Ūlā, 965: The Ḥanafī kadi rented from the Karaite Jewish physician 'Abd al-Karīm b. Mūsā, a room in a building that was part of the Karaite charitable endowment in al-Sharaf quarter. The annual rent will be one gold coin which he may spend on the necessary repairs.

6 (c) 11 Jumādā'l-'Ūlā, 965: The above-mentioned physician together with another Karaite Jew, 'Abd al-Raḥīm b. Faraj-Allah, acknowledged receipt of the sum of 70 *sulṭānī* gold coins that the Jew Hārūn b. Irwīl had owed them along with a third Jew on account of the purchase of a consignment of cloth.

6 (d) 12 Jumādā'l-'Ūlā, 965: The Jew Dā'ūd b. Ḥayyim sued the Jew Brāhīm b. Shabtūn for a debt outstanding for two and a half years. He claimed that he had lent him five *sulṭānī* gold coins in the Jewish neighborhood and two Jews testified in court in support of his claim. The kadi accepted their testimony and ruled in favor of the plaintiff.

51 (a) 7 Jumādā'l-Thānī, 965: The Jew Nasīm b. Shmū'īl accused the Jew Shmīla b. Abū Jūkār of having physically attacked and wounded him in the Jewish neighborhood near Ibrāhīm Kāstrū's house. Two Muslim witnesses testified in support of his claim thereupon the kadi convicted him.

68 (d) Saturday, 20 Jumādā'l-Thānī, 965: The Jewess Zubayda b. Sulaymān, wife of Ibrāhīm accused the Jew Shmū' īl b. Mūsā of having beaten her in her own house, then having admitted it publicly. Upon the defendant's denial she had three Muslim witnesses support her claim in court, whereupon the kadi convicted him.

84 (e) 1 Rajab, 965: The Jewess Nalnā (?) b. Rūbī came to the Mālikī kadi and asked that her husband divorce her

legally. She also conceded that she owed him 5 *sulṭānī* gold coins. The husband agreed and divorced her then and there.

100 (c) 9 Rajab, 965: The Jew Ibrāhīm b. Yūsif b. Mar'ī leased to the Jewess Sulṭānā b. Yūsif Zārkū a two-story house he owned in the Jewish neighborhood for the sum of 7 gold coins for a period of seven and a half years. Three gold coins out of the above he transferred to the Jewess Simḥa b. Ya'qūb for repairs that her husband, the former tenant, had made in the building.

119 (d) 22 Rajab, 965: The head of the Jewish community, Nassīm, pledged to refrain from drawing up any marriage contract among members of his community without the kadi's permission, nor will he hide any such marriage from him.

148 (b) 7 Sha'bān, 965: The Jewess Simḥa b. Mūsā accused her former husband, the Jew Mūsā b. al-Fatālī of not having paid her the outstanding debt of her dowry which amounted to 50 gold coins. The accused denied the allegation and produced two Jewish witnesses (names provided) who supported his claim that the sum in question was 40 coins which he had paid and at the time she had admitted receipt.

154 25 Ṣafar, 965: A text of a long *ḥujja* copied from the *sijill* of Cairo: A Jerusalemite Muslim alias Abū Zurayq al-Qudsī proved in court that the Rabbanite Jew Isḥāq b. 'Aṭiyya b. Sulaymān alias Shulāl, formerly the tax collector (*'āmil*) in Bāb al-Naṣr in Cairo, owed him 331 *dinār* gold coins. Since the debtor's death the guarantor of this debt, the Rabbanite Jew Isḥāq alias Mūlīnā the rabbi (*dayyān*) of the *'ifranj* community, should be held responsible. A lengthy debate follows in which false witnesses tried to establish the date of Shulāl's death on the wrong day but the kadi refuted their claim by checking the actual date at the *Dīwān al-'Ālī*[84] in Cairo.

158 (b) 12 Sha'bān, 965: The Jew Mināḥim b. Ma'tūq bought from Kasaba b. Ibrāhīm the blind Jewish cantor (*al-ḥazzān*) one quarter of a house he owned in

[84] *EI*^{2}, s.v. "Dīwān."

partnership with his two sisters in al-Rīsha quarter (*ḥāra*) "near the Jewish neighborhood (*maḥalla*)" (adjacent buildings detailed are also Jewish, including Ibrāhīm Kastrū's) for 25 *sulṭānī* gold coins.

158 (c) 12 Sha'bān, 965: Mināḥim b. Ma'tūq claimed a debt of 9 gold coins from Kasaba b. Ibrahīm alias "son of the cantor," which the defendant admitted.

158 (d) 12 Sha'bān, 965: The Jewess Sāra b. Yahūdā authorized the Muslim builder (*mi'mār*) to sue her former husband Shmū'īl b. Mūsā for her dowry and other legal rights for the sum of 75 gold coins.

231 (d) 27 Ramaḍān, 965: A Muslim and the expert Jewish saddle-maker (*sarrāj*), *mu'allim* Nassīm b. Yūsif, agreed in court that the latter owed the former 32 *sulṭānī* gold coins as the last installment of earlier debts.

233 (f) 28 Ramaḍān, 965: The Moroccan Jewess Amīra b. 'Abd-Allah the public-crier (*dallāla*) declared that she would guarantee all monetary obligations of her son Ya'qūb b. Isrā'īl vis-a-vis his wife Stīr b. Ya'qūb b. 'Aṭiyya.

242 (b) 5 Ramaḍān, 965: The Jew Hārūn b. Ilyā accused the Jew Faraj-Allah b. 'Abd-Allah of not having honored a debt of 6 *sulṭānī* gold coins he had lent him "during their holiday." Upon denial, the plaintiff produced two Jewish witnesses ('Āzir b. Ibrahīm and Mūsā b. Isḥaq) then the kadi ruled in his favor.

280 (b) 1 Shawwāl, 965: The Jew Ibrahīm b. Yāsif reported that he owned a house in the Jewish quarter (*ḥāra*) which was in a dilapidated state. He asked for a permit to reconstruct it, so the kadi sent his scribe to check the facts. The latter reported that the upper floor of the house was actually in ruins whereupon the kadi issued the requested permit.

316 (d) 22 Dhū'l-Qa'da, 965: The inspector of the markets (*muḥtasib*) complained to the kadi of the scarcity of meat in the market "because of the slaughtering of the Jews" every day instead of the authorized Mondays and

Thursdays only. The kadi reiterated the regulation that in times of scarcity they should abide by the above restriction. Hence they should discontinue their daily slaughtering immediately.

398 (c) 1 Ṣafar, 966: Shmūʾīl b. Mūsā the Jewish weaver acknowledged the debt of 600 silver coins to a high-ranking officer in the Citadel in return for a consignment of 60 *mudd* of sesame.

419 (a) 13 Ṣafar, 966: The heads of the Jewish community (Yāsif b. Yaʿqūb the Egyptian rabbi, Salamūn b. Mūsā Shulāl, ʿĀzir b. Ibrahīm and Hārūn b. Ilyā) asked the high-ranking official (*kātib al-wilāya al-sharīfa*), who arrived from Damascus for land registration purposes, to establish the territorial boundaries of the plot they had been using to bury their dead, as well as the amount of rent they had to pay for its use. A fact-finding committee of high-ranking military officers was sent and inspected the site (lengthy descriptions follow of the "old" and the "new" boundaries, as well as the names and titles of the officers involved). Pursuant to their report a decision was taken by the kadi as to the actual sum the Jews would have to pay annually for the lease.

434 (a) 17 Ṣafar, 962: The Jewess Qamar, wife of Yūsif the Jewish spice dealer, deposited several pieces of jewelry and other personal effects with the *muḥtasib* (a detailed list provided) authorizing him to hand them over to her creditor (a high-ranking officer in the Citadel) in the event that she would be absent from Jerusalem. A rider to the above document indicates that the officer actually received these items.

467 (c) 21 Rabīʿ al-Awwal, 961: An agreement of mutual absolution from any outstanding debts or obligations between the kadi and the Jews Mūsā and his wife.

Volume 37
(1559)

27 (b) 8 Rabīʻ al-Awwal, 966: Krārā b. Shmū'īl, a Jewish seamstress, is accused by a Muslim customer of having miscalculated the amount of cloth needed to sew him a garment.

127 (c) 26 Jumādā'l-'Ūlā, 966: The Jews Salamūn b. Mūsā and Isḥāq b. Ibrāhīm rented the bakery in front of the synagogue for a year.

127 (d) 26 Jumādā'l-'Ūlā, 966: The above-mentioned bakery was leased by the above-mentioned Salamūn and Isḥāq to a Muslim for a higher rent.

163 (b) 21 Jumādā'l-Thānī, 966: The Jew Nassīm b. Yūsif the saddler admitted that his outstanding debt to a Muslim amounted to 13 gold coins and 30 silver coins. His two wives (one of whom is black, *al-ḥabashiyya*) guaranteed this debt and even provided a mortgage to ensure it.

267 (h-l) 10 Rajab, 966: Yūsif b. ʻAbd al-Karīm, the head of the Jewish community (*shaykh al-yahūd*), guaranteed a long list of different Jewish people in a case of the burglary of Rabbi Dā'ūd's house.

286 (g) 7 Sha'bān, 966: The Jew Simḥa, living in Safed, owed a sum of money to several Muslim orphans.

287 (a) 7 Sha'bān, 966: Other amounts of money are owed to the above-mentioned by Nassīm the saddler and Shmū'īl b. Falāq.

287 (b) 8 Sha'bān, 966: A Muslim leased the mill in the Jewish quarter.

382 (b) 16 Ramaḍān, 966: The distinguished members (*a'yān*)[85] of the silversmiths' guild (2 Christian and 2 Jewish names provided) came to the court and requested that the Jew Mūsā b. Ibrāhīm be appointed head of the guild.

406 (b) The first third (*awā'il*) Shawwāl, 966: 11 Jews (names provided) acknowledge that their combined debt to the Christian Khalīl b. al-Qundulift amounts to 57 gold coins of which they already had paid him 10.

431 (a) 17 Shawwāl, 966: The Jewess Ḥannā b. Ya'qūb complained that her co-wife attacked and beat her.

431 (i) 17 Shawwāl, 966: The head of the Jewish community underwrote (*kafāla*) four Jews in the case of the belongings of a high official found in the vicinity of their houses.

477 (d-h) 16 Dhū'l-Qa'da, 966: The Jewish head of the silversmiths' guild, Mūsā b. Hārūn, complained that members of his guild have no one to guarantee them in case of faulty work, whereupon a Christian silversmith guaranteed separately several of his Christian peers.

478 (b) 17 Dhū'l-Qa'da, 966: Attempts by a variety of high officials to exact payments from the Jewish community for their lease of the cemetery on Mount of Olives (al-Jismāniyya).

516 (a) 8 Dhū'l-Ḥijja, 966: A Muslim dignitary claimed that the Jew Shmū'īl b. Yāsif owed him 106 silver coins. The latter's imprisonment in order to force him to pay his debt proved useless, since he was destitute. Upon evidence of his sad state he was released.

520 (a) 12 Dhū'l-Ḥijja, 966: The Jew Murdukhān b. Mināḥīm lent a Catholic woman 30 gold coins in Edirne, then hired her as a maid to his wife for the sum of 3 gold coins a year to be deducted from her debt. At the end of seven years he paid her the outstanding 9 coins and they acquitted one another.

---

[85] *EI*^{2}, s.v. "A'yān."

520 (b) 12 Dhū'l-Ḥijja, 966: The heads of the Jewish community undertook the payment of 45 gold coins to The Dome of the Rock endowment out of the inheritances of Jews living in Jerusalem. The entire sum will be divided into two six-month installments.

527 (e) 17 Dhū'l-Ḥijja, 966: The Jew Mūsā b. 'Āzir claimed that three other Jews attacked and beat him in the synagogue.

530 (c) 19 Dhū'l-Ḥijja, 966: The above-mentioned Mūsā is accused by the defendants in the above-mentioned case of an identical assault.

530 (d) 19 Dhū'l-Ḥijja, 966: Mūsā was accused–and found guilty–of having assaulted Zakarī b. Salamūn in the synagogue, yanking his headgear off his head and pulling his beard. Therupon he was sentenced and flogged.

Volume 38
(1570 - 1571)

133 (c) 1 Shawwāl, 978: The Jew Elīshū'a b. Ibrāhīm admitted at a court session conducted in the village of Sārīs that he was engaged in commercial relations with the Banū 'Aṭiyya bedouins. He actually showed the court the items (including rifles) he had purchased from these "rebellious bedouins."

133 (d) 1 Rabī' al-Awwal, 978: The Jew Aṣlān b. 'Amrān alias "Abū Karsha (Big Belly)" was accused by the *ṣūbashī* of the rural sub-district *(nāḥiya)* of Jerusalem of the conduct of commercial relations with the rebellious bedouins. He confessed and took out of his saddle a variety of items (including gunpowder) he had purchased from them. Thereupon he was convicted.

Volume 39
(1560 - 1563)

73 (a) 12 Rabīʻ al-Thānī, 970: The Rabbanite Jew Ibrāhīm b. Mūsā gave a deposition in court enumerating all his belongings, adding that he owed nothing to, and was entitled to nothing from, the merchant ʻĀzir b. Ibrahīm, or Jamīla b. Mūsā the wife of Aṭlāwī the rabbi (*al-dayyān*), or any other member of his community.

98 (a) 15 Rabīʻ al-Thānī, 967: The kadi fixed the annual rent to be paid by the Jewish community for the use of the land of their cemetery (details of location provided) at 100 *qubruṣī* gold coins. He formulated his assessment after having consulted a variety of religious dignitaries (names and titles provided) and having taken into account the desecration of the soil as a result of the ongoing burials therein.

173 (b) 20 Jumādā'l-Awwal, 967: A group of Jews living (*mustawṭinīn*) in Jerusalem complained of the Jew Yamṭūf b. Masʻūd. These were Salamūn b. Mūsā Shulāl, Ibrāhīm b. Hilāl, Saʻīd b. ʻĀzir, Yūsif b. ʻĀbd al-Karīm and Hārūn b. Liyāhū Malkī–all of whom stated that he had been selling them *'iṭreyf* meat although this was forbidden as far as their religion was concerned. Thereupon he declared that he would never again slaughter, skin or sell any meat to members of his community.

253 (b) 27 Jumādā'l-Thānī, 967: A Moslem accused the Jew ʻĀzir b. Mūsā of not having paid for a consignment of grapes he had sold him.

253 (d) 27 Jumādā'l-Thānī, 967: The *sipāhī* officer in charge of the village of Silwān demanded that the head of the Jewish community, Yūsif b. ʻAbd al-Karīm and another Jew, Hārūn b. Ilyās, pay him for the tithe (*ʻushr*) of the land they have been using for their cemetery in the Kidron valley (*wādī jahannam*). A debate followed as

to the exact sum they owed, then the kadi ruled in accordance with the lower rate they stated.

319 (b) 9 Sha'bān, 967: The kadi established the annual rate of 100 gold coins to be paid by the Jewish community to the charitable endowment of al-Ṣalāḥiyya for the lease of their cemetery located at Gethsemane. This figure was reached after a thorough and detailed inspection by a long list of Muslim experts. A description of the location and a list of names of the many distinguished experts consulted are provided.

369 (e) 2 Ramaḍān, 967: The following Jews came to the court: Salamūn b. Mūsā Shulāl, Ibrāhīm b. Hilāl, Sa'īd b. 'Āzir, Yūsif b. 'Ābd al-Karīm, Hārūn b. Ilyā and Malkī. They formally authorized Yamṭūf b. Mas'ūd to skin the slaughtered beasts as well as sell the non-Kosher (*al-'iṭreyf*) meat in their neighborhood in accordance with their traditional custom.

384 (b) 26 Dhū'l-Qa'da, 970: An agreement of mutual release between a Muslim woman and the Jewish *'ifranjī* master (*al-mu'allim*) tailor Isḥaq b. Ibrāhīm. She acknowledged receipt of all his rent for the house he had leased from her in the Jewish neighborhood (bordering the Temple Mount, *al-ḥaram al-sharīf,* on the building's eastern flank ?– A.C.).

384 (c) 5 Dhū'l-Qa'da, 970: The Jewish "master" (*al-mu'allim*) Mūshī b. Zimrā authorized his son-in-law (*khatanahu zawj ibnatihi*) Mūshī Bashkīr to fully represent him in any lawsuit or other financial matter that might eventuate concerning any person.

408 (c) 18 Ramaḍān, 967: The *muḥtasib* brought Yahūdā b. Mūsā the blacksmith to court and accused him of selling apples at his home as well as of using faulty scales.

429 (a) 4 Shawwāl, 967: The distinguished Shāfi'ī *shaykh* who served as a comptroller (*nāẓir*) and teacher at al-Ṣalāḥiyya *madrasa* sued several Jewish dignitaries for allegedly unauthorized use of the plot they took as their cemetery. The accused were Malkī b. Yahūdā, Mūsā b. Ḥayyim, 'Āzir b. Ibrāhīm, Salamūn b. Mūsā

Shulāl, Yūsif b. ʻĀbd al-Karīm, ʻAbd al-Laṭīf the Karaite physician, Isḥaq b. Ibrahīm, Dā'ūd b. Dmīrū' and Yūsif b. Yaʻqūb the Egyptian rabbi (*dayyān*). When the first two introduced an official document authorizing them and a third Jew to lease it (the plot) for thirty years for that specific purpose, it transpired that the third lease-holder had died. Thereupon the kadi ruled that one third of the lease should be cancelled.

431-433 4 Shawwāl, 967: A very long and detailed description of the vicissitudes of the Jewish community's lease of their cemetery at the Gethsemane endowment on the Mount of Olives, including names of community leaders (e.g. Dā'ūd b. Zmīrū'), texts of legal opinions (*fatwā*), changing lease rates, official Ottoman involvement, etc.

447 (b) 10 Shawwāl, 967: The heads of the Jewish community (names provided, including the two rabbis, Dā'ūd b. Zmīrū' and Yūsif Karakūz) were sued by the Ottoman cavalry officer (*sipāhī*) who had been granted the fief of the village Silwān. According to him they owed him the tithe tax (*ʻushr*) due from their cemetery which constituted part of his *tīmār* fief. The defendants confirmed his claim, hence it was ruled that this should be subtracted from the annual lease they paid to al-Ṣalāḥiyya charitable endowment.

457 (b) 16 Shawwāl, 967: Former court decisions on the rate to be paid by the Jewish community for lease of their cemetery are being sent to The Sublime Porte in Istanbul for review.

487 (a) 8 Dhū'l-Qaʻda, 967: An earlier ruling that was given by the Shāfiʻī kadi in the month of Ṣafar is reproduced here stating that the rate of the lease of the Jewish community for their cemetery had been 100 gold coins per year for 30 consecutive years. It was based on the testimonies of several Muslims from neighboring villages. The Ḥanbalī as well as the Ḥanafī kadis also attached their seals to further sanction that ruling.

519 (b) The last third (*awākhir*) of Dhū'l-Qaʻda, 967: A long list of the belongings of the Egyptian rabbi, Yūsif Karakūz, compiled after his death by the Muslim high-ranking

official in charge of the "treasury" (*bayt al-māl)* of all heirless legacies.

525 (i) 22 Sha'bān, 970: The Karaite Jew in charge of the imperial mint in Damascus, also served as the comptroller (*nāẓir*) of the Karaite charitable endowment in Jerusalem. He delegated this latter authority to "the master" (*al-mu'allim*) Karaite Jew Ibrahīm b. Faraj-Allah in Jerusalem and received the kadi's sanction for this.

580 (a) 5 Muḥarram, 968: The kadi cancels an earlier decision that granted the high-ranking cavalry officer in charge of the fief (*tīmār*) of Silwān the tithe accruing from the lease of the Jewish cemetery. This tithe should actually be paid to the governor of the District of Jerusalem (*mīr līwā'*) since it is part of his appanage, as is specifically stated in the new register of the imperial land registration (*taḥrīr*).

643 On the inside of the binding several disjointed notes, one of which reports the death of the Egyptian rabbi Yūsif b. Karakūz on Friday, 23 Dhū'l-Qa'da, 967.

Volume 40
(1561)

124 (d) 28 Rabīʻ al-Thānī, 968: The Jew "master" (*al-muʻallim*) Yaʻqūb b. Ibrahīm al-Sukkarī acknowledged that he owed the charitable endowment of The Dome of the Rock he sum of 70 gold coins for the lease of all income from Jewish pilgrims and inhabitants that would accrue to the "treasury" of Jewish heirless inheritances (*bayt māl ṭā'ifat al-yahūd)* for the duration of one year. This will include the 25 gold coins already pledged by the former lease holder for the same year.

125 (a) 28 Rabīʻ al-Thānī, 968: The above-mentioned Yaʻqūb acknowledged receipt of the above 15 (referred to there as 25) gold coins from the two Jews (one of whom is the head of the community) who had formerly taken the same lease (*muqā ṭaʻa*) having undertaken to pay a lower sum than originally pledged.

125 (b) 28 Rabīʻ al-Thānī, 968: The heads of the Jewish community stated in court that they would not be held responsible for the above pledge of Yaʻqūb. He was then asked to produce a guarantor for the sum, and he brought a Muslim person who provided the required guarantee.

125 (c) 28 Rabīʻ al-Thānī, 968: The above Yaʻqūb sued the two Jews who had been leasing the above *bayt al-māl* for the past 4 years. They proved in court that their lease was adequate and formally authorized, at the annual rate of 45 gold coins, hence his accusation was clearly inadmissible.

139 (b) 6 Jumādā'l-Awwal, 968: The Jew Yūsif b. Mināḥim stated in court the various amounts of money that he owed his wife and other Jews, as well as a consignment of olive oil deposited with him by a Jewish woman. The statement was made in the presence of the Muslim high official in charge of the "treasury" of Jewish inheritances as well as that of the Jew who actually

managed it (the same Ya'qūb referred to in the documents cited above).

142 (a) The first third (*awā'il)* of Jumādā'l-Awwal, 968: The above-mentioned Jew gave a very detailed statement of all his belongings in the presence of the above-mentioned officials.

160 (i) 21 Jumādā'l-Awwal, 968: The Jew Ya'qūb b. Ibrāhīm leased to his Muslim guarantor half the lease of the income of the "treasury" of Jewish inheritances for half the annual sum that he actually paid.

186 (e) 5 Jumādā'l-Thānī, 968: The head of the Jewish community, Yūsif b. 'Abd al-Karīm, was granted the lease of the "treasury" of Jewish inheritances for the annual sum of 71 gold coins which amounted to an increase of one gold coin over and above the sum pledged by the former Muslim lease-holder.

186 (f) 5 Jumādā'l-Thānī, 968: A Muslim sued a Jewish tailor who allegedly received a piece of cloth from him, but failed to deliver the garment he had promised (to sew).

Volume 42
(1556)

123[86] The first third (*awā'il*) of Rajab, 963: A Sultanic decree addressed to the governor of Damascus and the kadis of Damascus, Gaza and Jerusalem. The Jews of Cairo, Damascus, Jerusalem and Safed submitted a petition describing acts of harassment perpetrated by the local authorities against Jewish pilgrims to Jerusalem and Hebron. Many false accusations are resorted to in order to extract unlawful fines from them. The Sultan decreed that a thorough investigation into this matter should be conducted, and if confirmed, this conduct should be discontinued.

---

[86] Turkish.

Volume 44
(1563)

401 (e) 1 Dhū'l-Ḥijja, 970: The Jewish slaughterer Yūsif b. Ibrāhīm was warned by the Ḥanafī kadi–who took action after a complaint was launched by some Shāfi'ī dignitaries–that he should not exercise his profession on any day other than Mondays and Thursdays.

401 (f) 1 Dhū'l-Ḥijja, 970: The head of the Jewish community (*shaykh al-yahūd*), Yūsif b. 'Abd al-Karīm, presented the court with a copy of an imperial order authorizing the Jews to slaughter any day they wish as long as this is done to fulfil an actual need in their community. Thereupon the kadi ruled that they may slaughter every day according to their needs, but in any event each day's slaughter should not exceed 3 sheep.

438 (a) 29 Shawwāl, 970: At the end of a complaint against the high-handed and immoral behavior of two Muslims, a detailed list appears of all those who supported it, i.e. the "dignitaries" (*a'yān*) of the seven neighborhoods (*maḥalla*) of Jerusalem, those of the Christians, then the Jewish "dignitaries and elders" (*akābir*): Mināḥim b. Ya'qūb, Mūsā b. Jūkār, his son Shamīla, Yūsif the sesame oil dealer (*sayrajānī*), his son Shamīla, Yūsif b. Mardūkh, his brother Sulaymān, Dā'ūd b. Ḥayyim, Isḥaq b. Ibrāhīm, Aṣlān Yahūdā, Salamūn b. Yūsif, Yūsif b. 'Abd al-Kar īm, Salamūn b. Sūmān, Rāḥamīn, Shū'a b. Manṣūr.

448 (d) 8 Muḥarram, 971: 40 shops in "the new market," formerly known as "the vegetable market" (*sūq al-khuḍar*) were leased by the authorities of the charitable endowment of the Temple Mount to their respective Muslim, Christian and Jewish tenants for nine years. The latter group was comprised of Mūsā b. Malīḥa, Shalamūn b. Shulāl, his brother Liyā, Shalamūn b. Sūqān, Sa'īd, Ibrāhīm "the Kurd," Khalīfa b. Raqiyya, Mūsā b. Nūfā'īl, Sulaymān "the physician," Yūsif b.

'Abd al-Kar īm, his brother Ibrāhīm. This is the largest of the three groups that comprised 25 people altogether.

462 (d) Another copy of page 448 (d) of the *sijill.*

574 (b) 5 Rabī' al-Awwal, 971: The rabbi Dā'ūd b. Zm īr, the Ashkenazi (*al-amanī)* Dā'ūd Abū Sha'r and Salamūn the physician (*al-ṭabīb*) paid 200 gold coins to the endowment of the seminary (*madrasa*) of al-Ṣalāḥiyya for the lease of their cemetery for two years. Present also in court were the Jews Ibrāhīm b. 'Abd al-Karīm, Salamyā Isḥaq, Dā'ūd the jeweler, Yahūdā the blacksmith, the Karaite Ibrāhīm, the Ashkenazi (*al-amanī*) Aṣlān Yahūdā, 'Āzir the cloth merchant (*jawkhī*), Salamūn b. Shulāl and Yūsif b. 'Abd al-Karīm.

574 (c-d) 5 Rabī' al-Awwal, 971: More on the lease of the Jewish cemetery.

Volume 45
(1563 - 1564)

23 (c) 16 Rabī‘ al-Ākhir, 971: The dignitaries (*a‘yān*) of the Jewish community were summoned to court to be told by the kadi that upon the death of a member of their community they must divide his belongings among his heirs according to the Islamic law after proper notification of the authorities, while special attention should be paid to avoid any infringment of the rights of the young ones.

136 (f) The last third (*awākhir*) of Jumādā'l-Ākhir, 971: The Karaite Jewish jeweler Ibrāhīm b. Faraj Allah purchased from a Muslim an orchard (*ghirās*) of grapes, figs, almonds and olives located at the endowment of Aḥmad al-Thawrī outside of Jerusalem. The price paid: 20 gold coins.

161 (a) 21 Rajab, 971: The dignitaries of the Jewish community leased from the Muslim kadi in charge of an endowment (name missing in the original document, probably that of Aḥmad al-Thawrī) a plot of land outside of Jerusalem and used it as a Jewish cemetery.

221 (a) 12 Ramaḍān, 971: A delegation of spice dealers (*‘aṭṭār*) consisting of Muslims, Christians and Jews (the latter: Salamūn b. Shulāl and Ibrāhīm b. Hilāl) complained to the court of the high-handed behaviour of the inspector of the markets (*muḥtasib*) against them. The court reiterated an earlier imperial decree forbidding the *muḥtasib* from any interference in the trade or business in the spice dealers' market.

244 (e) 3 Shawwāl, 971: An imperial decree forbids any attempt by the military authorities in Jerusalem to exact unlawful taxes from Jewish pilgrims who come from Cairo or Damascus and who wish to visit the holy places in the vicinity of Jerusalem.

Volume 46
(1565)

92 (d) 14 Jumādā'l-Awwal, 972: Salamūn b. Mūsā Shulāl, the head of the Jewish community, presented the court with a document (*raj'a*) stating full payment of the poll tax for 90 people of the Jewish community for the year 972. It was issued by the high-ranking official (*amīn*) in charge of all Imperial Domains income.

123 (c) 1 Jumādā'l-Thānī, 972: 13 Jews (names provided) complained at court of the misbehaviour of Sulaymān, the Jewish physician, and asked that he be expelled from their neighborhood.

124 (d) 1 Jumādā'l-'Ūlā, 972: Hārūn b. Bayrām, a Jewish doctor from Safed, rented a house in the street leading to *Bāb al-Silsila* gate for a year for the amount of 100 silver coins.

146 (e) 7 Rajab, 972: The kadi warned several spice dealers (the Christian Khalīl al-Qundulift, the Jewish Yūsif b. 'Abd al-Karīm and Salamūn b. Mūsā Shulāl) that they must get themselves a head for their guild, as well as a public-crier (*dallāl*).

152 (e) The second third (*awāsiṭ*) of Rajab, 972: A Muslim dignitary from al-Ḥusaynī family rented a house from the Karaite endowment located at the eastern side of the Karaite neighborhood for 3 years. The rent: 3 gold coins per year.

184 (d) 5 Sha'bān, 972: The Karaite Yahūdā b. 'Abd al-Karīm rented all the shops located in the Jewish quarter near the gate of "the big market" (*al-sūq al-kabīr*) for three years. The rent: 3 gold coins per year.

Volume 47
(1560 - 1564)

11[87] 23 Rabīʻ al-Awwal, 972: A diploma (*berāt*) appointing a Jewish physician from Istanbul to practice medicine in Jerusalem. A fixed daily salary is allocated by the Sultan to remunerate him for all medical services rendered there.

33[88] 1 Dhū'l-Qaʻda, 967: A Sultanic decree based on a petition sent by the Jews of Jerusalem forbids any further harassment of the Jewish butchers by the *muḥtasib*. It was reported that he ruled against all slaughtering of sheep for Muslim customers by Jewish slaughterers and the sale of meat slaughtered by Jews at the Muslim butcher shops. A legal opinion (*fatwā*) of the chief *muftī* of Istanbul is cited to the effect that meat slaughtered by Jews may be consumed by Muslims, and the local authorities should not interfere or try to stop it.

---

[87] Turkish.
[88] Turkish.

Volume 48
(1565 - 1566)

51 (a) 9 Shawwāl, 972: The Jew Shmū'īl b. Abū Jūkār reported the loss of a donkey that had been kept in his home; then it was spotted in the possession of a Muslim peasant. When he tried to question him (the peasant) the latter escaped. Hence the Jew asked and was granted the court's permission to take possession of the donkey pending final decision.

185 (e) 26 Muḥarram, 973: The Jew Yahūdā b. Sa'īd sued the Jew Mūsā b. Nassīm for a debt, part of which the accused admitted. The kadi ruled that he pay this part pending further proof to be presented to the court.

196 (b) 7 Ṣafar, 973: The following Jews were recognized by the kadi as entitled to provide the town with grains (*ḥidāra*): Ibrāhīm b. *al-najjār* ("son of the carpenter"); Shmū'īl b. Tammām; Shū'a b. Sabtūn; Shmū'īl "the tinner" (*al-mubayyiḍ*); Hārūn "the Moroccan" (*al-maghribī*); Yūsif b. Isḥaq "the apricot" (*barqūq*) from Kafr Kannā; Shū'a the Nabulsi; Nassīm b. Dā'ūd; Farrūj b. 'Abd-Allah.

208 (g) 16 Ṣafar, 973: Isḥaq b. Mūsā declared in court that he left the Jewish religion and adopted Islam.

215 (d) 21 Ṣafar, 973: A Jewish convert to Islam sold to the Jew Yūsif b. 'Abd al-Karīm several items that pertain to Jewish matters.

225 (e) 2 Rabī' al-Awwal, 973: The Jewess Fraykha b. Rūbīn declared that her mother had given her a long list of pieces of jewelry (details provided) for safe-keeping as well as for her own use.

279 (c) 5 Rabī' al-Thānī, 973: The Jew Ibrāhīm b. Sabtūn was obligated by the kadi to pay the Jew Yahūdā b. Mūsā a debt he owed him for a consignment of wheat they owned in partnership.

325 (b) The first third (*awā'il*) of Jumādā'l-Awwal, 973: The Jew Ibrāhīm b. Hilāl leased from the Muslim deputy comptroller of a charitable endowment two shops in the spice dealers' market (*sūq al-'aṭṭārīn*). Both shops are flanked by shops leased to Muslims and the lease was taken for one year.

340 (d) 23 Jumādā'l-Awwal, 973: A Muslim sued the Jewess Klāra b. Shmū'īl for a piece of silk he allegedly left with her to be sewn. She gave the court a sworn testimony to the effect that it had been stolen from her house one night along with other items and the kadi ruled in her favor.

369 (b) 12 Jumādā'l-Thānī, 973: The high official in charge of the collection of poll tax in the province of Damascus sent a janissary to Jerusalem in order to check on the actual number of Jews liable for payment of this tax. He reported that he had found no individuals, either among the Jerusalem community or those originally from Kafr Kannā, in addition to those registered earlier.

369 (c) 12 Jumādā'l-Thānī, 973: More on the actual collection of poll tax from the Jewish community.

372 (d) 12 Jumādā'l-Thānī, 973: A Christian monk representing the Greek Orthodox Patriarch accused Ibrāhīm b. Faraj Allah, the Jewish money changer (*ṣayrafī*) for the high official in charge of the collection of poll tax in the province of Damascus, as well as the janissary he sent to Jerusalem, of extortion. The latter confessed and returned his share while the Jew denied the allegation. When the plaintiff produced two reliable Muslim witnesses the Jew was arrested pending payment of his share.

465 (e) 17 Ramaḍān, 973: Yaḥyā, a Jewish physician in Jerusalem, received his daily salary (*'ulūfa*) from the dues levied by the inspector of the markets (*iḥtisāb*) of this town. It was computed for the entire year at the rate of 15 *'uthmānī* silver coins per day, as per specific orders to this effect sent from Damascus.

467 (a) 17 Ramaḍān, 973: The Jewish cloth merchant Ilyās b. Ibrāhīm was paid in kind by the scribe (*yāzijī*) of the governor of Jerusalem by way of defraying a debt that the governor owed him on account of a cloth transaction as well as an earlier loan. He agreed to receive a consignment of alkali and of olive oil, the total value of which amounted to three hundred and eighty-one and a half *sulṭānī* gold coins.

Volume 49
(1566 - 1567)

5	(b)	Last day of Ramaḍān, 973: A balance sheet of the inspection of the markets (*iḥtisāb*) lease for one year, including an entry that reads: "the salary of the Jewish doctor, 65 gold coins and 30 silver coins."
14	(e)	5 Shawwāl, 973: The income of *bayt māl al-yahūd* ("the treasury of [heirless deceased] Jews"), originally leased to the Jew Isḥāq b. Ibrāhīm, was now granted to a Muslim for 3 years; he paid 25 percent more for the lease.
60	(e)	23 Dhū'l-Qa'da, 973: Yahūdā b. Sa'īd, the Jewish slaughterer, is warned that he should altogether avoid mixing meat slaughtered by him and that slaughtered by Muslims. The warning was a result of complaints submitted by Muslims.
78	(h)	15 Dhū'l-Ḥijja, 973: The Jewish doctor Yaḥyā confirms receipt of 800 silver coins from the *muḥtasib* of Jerusalem.
125	(a)	The last third (*awākhir*) of Muḥarram, 974: The Christian and Jewish silversmiths (names provided) agreed to choose one of them for head of their guild. His main responsibilities are detailed.
179	(d)	25 Rabī' al-Awwal, 974: Two Jewish men and two women (names provided) swore that they had not touched the belongings of the deceased Jewish doctor, Yaḥyā.
184	(a)	27 Rabī' al-Awwal, 974: The Jew Isḥāq b. Ibrāhīm was established as a proxy (*wakīl*) of a Jewish woman, Rāḥīl b. Ya'qūb, who was the mother of a deceased Jewish doctor, Yaḥyā b. Yūsif b. Salamūn.
203	(b)	21 Rabī' al-Ākhir, 974: One of the Muslim notables (*a'yān*) of Jerusalem purchased from the Jew

al-mu'allim Yahūdā b. Mināḥim a house the latter had inherited 40 years earlier in the Jewish quarter near the city gate.

251 (c) 25 Jumādā'l-Awwal, 974: A Jewish woman, Qamar b. Sulaymān, collects a debt from the Jew Ya'qūb b. Yūsif out of a sum of money deposited with him by her husband.

289 (f) 23 Jumādā'l-Thānī, 974: Complaints against the *muḥtasib* of Jerusalem and his attempts to stop the Jewish community from slaughtering according to their own tradition.

294 (i) 27 Jumādā'l-Thānī, 974: A complaint of the Jewish wheat-merchants (*ḥaddār*) against attempts of the night-watches (*'asas*) to interfere with their import of grains from the surrounding villages.

306 (a) 11 Rajab, 974: A Muslim dignitary rented the mill located in the Jewish quarter.

312 (e) 10 Rajab, 974: A committee was sent by the court to verify a request of members of the Jewish community (names provided) to rebuild a few walls of their synagogue that had collapsed. Permission was granted as a result of their report.

344 (b) 9 Sha'bān, 974: A fairly detailed description of the formulation proclaimed by a Jew who adopted Islam.

484 (a) 28 Dhū'l-Qa'da, 974: The Jew Mūsā b. Isḥāq stated in court in the presence of his mother Ḥannā b. Ibrāhīm that a house adjacent to the synagogue to its south and to the "monastery of the Ashkenazis" (*dayr al-aman*) to its east has been his undisputed property for more than 30 years.

484 (b) 28 Dhū'l-Qa'da, 974: The above-mentioned house was sold by the above-mentioned owner to a Muslim dignitary for 75 gold coins.

501 (d) 17 Dhū'l-Ḥijja, 974: Two Muslim dignitaries purchased from the Jew Shmū'īl b. Sa'diyya b. Ibrāhīm half a

house in al-Rīsha quarter for 18 gold coins and a precious ring.

502 (a) End of the above document.

Volume 51
(1567 - 1569)

20 (a) 28 Rabīʿ al-Thānī, 975: A Muslim accused the Jew Masʿūd b. al-Fatālī of having improperly taken from his shop a certain amount of silver, whereas the defendant pleaded that he had given him that silver to deliver to a certain Jewish woman.

20 (h) 29 Rabīʿ al-Thānī, 975: The Jew ʿAṭūn b. Masʿūd accused a Muslim from the village of Bayt Taʿmar of having stolen a sheep he owned and had left in the care of a shepherd. The defendant denied it, but when two Muslim witnesses attested to an earlier public admission he had made in the Jewish neighborhood, he was found guilty.

114 (g) 27 Rajab, 975: The Jewish tanner Murdakhāy b. Yaʿqūb bought his brother's share in a house in the Jewish quarter (description provided) that they had inherited from their father.

223 (d) 25 Dhū'l-Qaʿda, 975: The Jew Salamūn b. Yūsif accused the Jew ʿĀzir b. Ibrāhīm of having attacked and beaten him in the spice dealers' market (*sūq al-ʿaṭṭārīn*). Several Muslim witnesses testified in support of the plaintiff's claim hence the defendant was sentenced to flagellation (*taʿzīr*) and the sentence was summarily carried out.

402 (d) 27 Jumādā'l-Awwal, 976: The Jew Shamīla b. Yūsif reported to the court that another Jew, Manḥūna b. Maʿtūf wished to make a legal statement of all his belongings before he died. The kadi sent a representative who recorded an inventory of all that belonged to that person (a detailed list of clothes, household effects and monetary debts provided). Manḥūna declared that the house he was living in was part of a charitable endowment that intended to support "the Jewish beggars." His two Jewish wives confirmed

the sums of money he owed them as part of their dowries.

485 (d) 9 Sha'bān, 976: In court the head of the Jewish community produced an imperial order to the effect that the Jewish community is authorized to slaughter in the slaughterhouse of Jerusalem without any harassment whatsoever. Now the *muḥtasib* of Jerusalem was trying to levy "the stamp tax" (*resm-i damga*) from the slaughterers. The kadi acknowledged the Jewish claim and warned the *muḥtasib* against any similar behaviour in the future.

650 (a) 27 Dhū'l-Ḥijja, 976: The Jewess Ḥilwa b. Ibrāhīm, wife of Ilyās b. Ibrāhīm, sued the Muslim scribe of the Citadel for a debt he owed her late husband. After her claim was confirmed by two high-ranking Muslim officials, the kadi ruled that he was obliged to pay her.

Volume 53
(1569 - 1570)

18 (b) 1 Jumādā'l-Thānī, 977: A Jewish seamstress was given a piece of cloth bought from a Jewish cloth merchant but she left for Safed before finishing work for a Muslim customer who insists that he should get the cloth back.

55 (a) 17 Rajab, 977: The Jewish doctor Dā'ūd b. Shūbā accused the Jew Salamūn b. Ṣūfān of having sent a soldier who forced him to return when he was on his way to Egypt.

55 (b) 18 Rajab, 977: The Jewish saddler and the Jewish cobbler were accused by several distinguished members of the community (names provided) of having performed an unsatisfactory job while digging graves for deceased Jews.

62 (b) 21 Rajab, 978: The Jew Sulaymān b. Shmū'īl requested and received a permit to rebuild parts of his house in the Jewish quarter, particularly its dilapidated roof.

131 (a) 2 Ramaḍān, 977: The Jew Yantūb b. Mūsā requested permission to rebuild his house in the Jewish quarter. A fact-finding committee sent by the kadi checked the particulars and gave a report, whereupon his request was granted.

131 (d) The first third (*awā'il*) of Ramaḍān, 977: The head of the Jewish community, Shamīla, paid the poll tax due from 90 people for the year 977.

161 (a) 21 Ramaḍān, 977: The distribution of a Jewish inheritance between the two Jewish heirs.

161 (b-c) 21 Ramaḍān, 977: More on the above-mentioned inheritance and several changes made in the relevant house.

193 (b) 16 Shawwāl, 977: The Jew Ya'qūb b. Mūsā from Safed, his mother and step-mother, his sister and his aunt, appointed another Jew from Safed as their proxy for a loan from two Jerusalemite Muslim merchants. In return for 227 gold coins they borrowed, the family mortgaged a house in al-Sharaf quarter.

194 (a) 16 Shawwāl, 977: Another official document describing the above-mentioned mortgage.

200 (c) The second third (*awāsiṭ*) of Shawwāl, 977: The Jew Yūsif b. Isḥāq b. Mūghān mortgaged his house in the Jewish quarter for a debt of 30 gold coins he owed a Muslim endowment. Said sum included 6 gold coins he owed for a robe (*qaftān*) of yellow Damascene silk he had bought and received.

212 (d) 28 Shawwāl, 977: The Egyptian Jewish physician Binyamīn b. Murād (?) b. Yahūdā declared just before his death that he owed his wife 30 gold coins as part of her bride money (*muhr*).

339 (b) 12 Muḥarram, 978: The Muslim comptroller (*nāẓir*) of al-Manāra endowment accused the two heads of the Jewish community of having unlawfully taken possession of 4 shops in the Jewish quarter. The latter confirmed the facts, but claimed all 4 were purchased by an Egyptian Jew who later endowed them.

356 (d) 22 Muḥarram, 978: The Jewish community leaders deny the allegation that they dispose of their garbage on a rubbish heap (*tall*) in the Jewish quarter.

371 (a) The last day of Muḥarram, 978: A Jewish woman declared in court that all she owned were the clothes she wore in the Jewish hospice known as the Ashkenazi monastery (*dayr al-aman*).

371 (b) The last day of Muḥarram, 978: Another Jewish woman, Stīr b. Ya'qūb, declared her few personal belongings.

387 (b) 9 Ṣafar, 978: The head of the Jewish community showed the court an imperial decree authorizing the

three Jewish cheese-makers to sell their merchandise in the Jerusalem sub-district.

388 (b) 20 Ṣafar, 978: The clerk (*yāzijī*) of the Citadel of Jerusalem claimed that a Jewish blacksmith owed him 6 gold coins and 10 silver coins for several items he had sold him.

403 (c) 21 Ṣafar, 978: Three Jewish orphans sold an orchard they had inherited from their father on al-Shaykh Jarrāḥ land to the Jew Lāwī b. Shmū'īl and Sībūnā (?) b. Mūsā in Jerusalem.

479 (b) 10 Rabī' al-Thānī, 978: The *ṣūbashī* of Jerusalem warned the Jews and Christians there that they should not produce wine unless they were authorized by the kadi to do so.

533 (d) 16 Jumādā'l-Awwal, 978: A dispute between the Jew Faraj-Allah al-Jawjalī and a janissary officer over the right to draw water from a water-cistern. The court upheld the Jewish claim.

Volume 54
(1571 - 1572)

24 (b) 23 Sha'bān, 978: The Jewish *dayyān* Yūsif b. Ibrāhīm applied for a permit to repair his house in the Jewish quarter. After a detailed inspection by a fact-finding committee, permission was granted by the kadi.

92 (c) 9 Shawwāl, 978: The Jewish physician Kamāl b. Mūsā leased a shop in the spice dealers' market that had been leased by a deceased Muslim physician. The rent was set at 5 silver coins per month.

102 (h) 21 Shawwāl, 978: The Jewish silversmith Mas'ūd b. al-Fatālī accused the head of the night-watches (*'ases bāshī*), holding him–as well as the actual watchman on duty–responsible for a burglary in his shop in the silversmiths' market (*sūq al-ṣāgha*). A long list of stolen goods is provided.

181 (b) 18 Dhū'l-Ḥijja, 978: The Jew Hārūn b. Yahūdā admitted that he owed a Muslim 100 silver coins.

181 (f) 19 Dhū'l-Ḥijja, 978: The Jewish chief (*al-rayyis*) physician, Kamāl b. Mūsā, along with several other Jewish leaders, provided the court with the names of the three Jewish slaughterers they authorized to serve the community.

261 (c) 22 Ṣafar, 979: The head of the physicians' guild, the Jew Kamāl b. Mūsā, before leaving Jerusalem for Cairo, applied for permission to appoint a substitute for his absence. The court granted him permission to leave for 3 months, and declared a Muslim physician as his replacement.

283 (c) 10 Rabī' al-Awwal, 979: A settlement of a debt between Shmū'īl b. Mūsā the Jew and Yahūdā b. Ibrāhīm b. Sanyūr (?) the broker (*simsār*).

334 (a) 26 Rabīʻ al-Thānī, 979: A detailed list of the belongings of a poor Jewish woman who asked on her death-bed that they be recorded.

432 (f) 5 Shaʻbān, 979: Several Jewish people accused the head of al-Rīsha quarter of extorting money from them on several occasions. The court addressed a similar question to Muslim merchants living in that quarter (and in the neighboring al-Sharaf quarter), and their answer was negative. A Christian supported the latter report.

436 (b) 8 Shaʻbān, 979: The head of the community Shamīla b. ʻUbayd the sesame oil dealer (*al-sayrajānī)*, claimed 30 gold coins from five Jews (names provided) on account of their poll tax which he had paid to the authorities. The defendants denied his allegation, admitted a debt of 18 gold coins, and were granted several days to bring forth their proofs.

440 (d) 15 Shaʻbān, 979: A Muslim sold to the Jew Isḥāq b. Sulaymān a house he had bought from the European Jew Shmūʼīl b. Yaʻqūb b. Ibrāhīm for the sum of 35 gold coins.

468 (e) 11 Ramaḍān, 979: The Jew Yaʻqūb b. Faraj-Allah came to the court escorted by one of the governor's officers and proclaimed that he had left his former religion and turned Muslim.

484 (b) 22 Ramaḍān, 979: The Jew Isḥāq b. Mūghān was convicted of publicly drinking wine in spite of explicit warnings not to.

521 (d) 22 Shawwāl, 979: An official inquiry was held to establish the cause and circumstances of the death of a three-year-old Jewish boy at his home. The mother reported that he had fallen into a deep well in the basement after he had seen her fetching water from it.

558 (c) 18 Shaʻbān, 979: A settlement was reached between the Muslim endowment administrator and the Jew Isḥāq b. Mūghān regarding an old debt of 36 gold coins.

Volume 55
(1572 - 1573)

58 (b) 7 Muḥarram, 980: The Jewish spice dealer Yahūdā b. Mūsā b. al-Ḥaddād and the Ashkenazi (*al-amanī*) Jewess Bīlā b. Sham'ūn submitted confirmation of mutual consent to a deal reached several months earlier in which the former acquired from the latter a small house (*duwayra)* in the Jewish quarter, located within a compound (*ḥawsh*) that belonged to a Jewish money changer. The sum of 40 gold coins was paid for this house that included a small court-yard with a pond, as well as a small vineyard.

58 (c) 7 Muḥarram, 980: The above-mentioned Bīlā was accused of owing a debt to a Muslim woman. Since she acknowledged only one part of the debt it was ruled that she should pay only this part, pending further proof.

59 (b) 7 Muḥarram, 980: The above-mentioned Bīlā together with a Muslim "master" (*mu'allim*) acknowledge a debt they owe another Muslim. Bīlā stated that she had put up a certain amount of silk as collateral with their creditor.

60 (a) 8 Muḥarram, 980: The above-mentioned Bīlā admitted that she owed a Muslim 3 gold coins for 4 *mithqāl* of pearls she had bought from him. She was arrested pending payment of her debt.

61 (c) 9 Muḥarram, 980: The above-mentioned Bīlā sued a Muslim acting as a trustee for his wife for a debt incurred when the latter bought several items of clothing from her. The husband acknowledged the debt, whereupon the kadi ruled that Bīlā be paid as per her claim.

63 (d) 12 Muḥarram, 980: The above-mentioned Bīlā was found liable for a debt to a Muslim who had sold her a certain amount of cloth and she was therefore put under arrest.

64 (e) 12 Muḥarram, 980: The above-mentioned Bīlā was sued by a Muslim for several gold bracelets and an expensive garment (*kamkha*) she allegedly held as collateral against a debt of the daughter of the late governor of Jerusalem. When the defendant presented the court with a different version the kadi sent a fact-finding commission to the distinguished daughter's house to verify the case. The latter confirmed part of Bīlā's version, hence she was obliged to return the garment, while the bracelets would remain at her (Bīlā's) disposal pending defrayal of her debt.

65 (b) 12 Muḥarram, 980: The above-mentioned Bīlā admitted that she owed a distinguished Muslim woman a sum of money for some pearls she had bought from her. Thereupon she was put under arrest pending payment of her debt.

105 (d) 18 Ṣafar, 980: The Jew Ya'qūb b. 'Aṭiyya owed a Muslim, alias "the butcher's son" a sum of money for a consignment of hides he had sold him. His Jewish wife undertook to pay and actually did pay the outstanding debt.

123 (b) 5 Rabī' al-Awwal, 980: The above-mentioned Bīlā was sued by a Muslim who claimed that since he had paid her his debt she should give him back a silver anklet she was keeping as collateral. She acknowledged that the anklet was in her possession, but against a much higher sum of money that he owed her. Upon her oath, the kadi ruled that the entire sum be paid back, and only then would the collateral be returned.

131 (d) 12 Rabī' al-Awwal, 980: A Muslim sued the Jewess Bīlā b. Sham'ūn for a substantial amount of money she owed him in her capacity as a guarantor for a third person. She acknowledged the debt but claimed insolvency and was then arrested for a long period "in order to find out whether she was [just] stubborn or [really] poor." When she persisted she was again brought to the kadi who asked whether she could present the court with any proof of her situation. She was released in order to fetch such proof. (End of document missing.)

163 (f) 11 Rabīʿ al-Thānī, 980: A Muslim "master" (*muʿallim*) reached an agreement with three of the heads of the Jewish community (names provided) to postpone the payment of the debt they guaranteed for the above-mentioned Ashkenazi Bīlā (see above, *sijill* 55/59 (b)).

172 (a) 20 Rabīʿ al-Thānī, 980: The head of the Jewish community, Shamīla b. Jūkār, was accused by a representative of the *sūbāshī* of unauthorized production of wine. An inspector sent by the kadi came up with an earthenware jar full of newly fermented wine which Shamīla admitted that he had made.

207 (a) 28 Jumādā'l-'Ūlā, 980: The Jewish community of Jerusalem complained to the authorities in Damascus of the allegedly inflated figures of members of the community liable for payment of the poll tax . Over ten years before, when the numbers were established–their argument continued–they included pilgrims and other foreigners who later returned to their places of origin hence the total of 185 poll tax paying Jews was incorrect. Special orders were therefore issued in Damascus for the Jerusalem authorities to verify the actual number of Jews there, and this was implemented by the governor and other high officials who repeatedly checked attendance in the synagogue in unannounced and secret visits. The total figure they reached was 115.

207 (b) 29 Jumādā'l-'Ūlā, 980: A list compiled by the Muslim authorities totalling 115 full names of the Jewish male inhabitants of Jerusalem liable for poll tax.

208 (f) 29 Jumādā'l-'Ūlā, 980: The seven "heads" (*mashā'ikh*, names provided) of the Jewish community acknowledged a debt of 25 *sulṭānī* gold coins to the head of the "feudal" cavalry officers (*mīr alāy*) of the Jerusalem district.

325 (g) 28 Ramaḍān, 980: A Moroccan (*maghribiyya*) Jewess was appointed by the kadi as the formal custodian (*waṣiyya*) of her two young children.

330 (b) 29 Ramaḍān, 980: A Muslim sued the above-mentioned Jewess for the sum of 30 gold coins her deceased husband had owed him (most of it for a *qinṭār* of rice). Several pieces of her jewelry had been mortgaged to him against the debt which she tried to deny, but when Muslim witnesses confirmed the plaintiff's claim, the defendant agreed to let him have the mortgaged pieces in exchange for her husband's debt.

343 (a) 13 Ramaḍān, 980: The Jewish jeweler Mas'ūd b. Al-Fatālī was involved in the sale of a consignment of soap he owned, to a Muslim dealer who undertook to export it to Egypt. A detailed breakdown is provided of expenses incurred at the various stages of the transaction, as well as on the road from Jerusalem to Cairo.

369 (f) 29 Shawwāl, 980: The kadi appointed the Jewish cloth merchant Ḥaḍr b. Aṣlān as custodian of his three young brothers.

370 (c) 29 Shawwāl, 980: Two Jewish witnesses (names provided) attested in court to the appointment of the Jew Khaḍr b. Aṣlān as an agent (*wakīl*) by his brother, his mother and his father's second wife (names provided), for the collection of a debt owed by the governor of Jerusalem to Khaḍr's deceased father.

371 (e) 29 Shawwāl, 980: The above-mentioned debt was exceptionally high, i.e. 1250 *sulṭānī* gold coins incurred by the governor to the deceased Aṣlān, the Jewish cloth merchant. The governor had mortgaged a bathhouse in Nablus (known as *ḥammām al-bāshā*) and having now acknowledged the entire debt he repaid most of it in kind (48 *qinṭār* of soap at 25 gold coins each).

390 (d) 18 Dhū'l-Qa'da, 980: The above-mentioned consignment of soap was stored by the governor at a soap factory named after Ṭurghūd Aghā. Its new owner, after having been shown its exact location, opted to keep it at the same place.

448 (f) 16 Muḥarram, 981: Two Jewish brothers state the details of an outstanding debt between them.

448 (g) 16 Muḥarram, 981: A Jewish husband was cautioned that he should provide his wife with proper accommodation and all her needs, while the wife was warned to refrain from further cursing or hitting her husband.

511 (c) 20 Rabī' al-Awwal, 981: A Jew sued another Jew for an alleged debt which the defendant completely denied.

535 (i) 18 Rabī' al-Thānī, 981: The Jewish community was accused of disposing the trash of the soap factories and other rubbish along the city walls next to the gate of the Jewish quarter. The chief builder of Jerusalem confirmed that the rubbish thus heaped on both sides of the wall was harmful to the construction. The head of the Jewish community denied having any part in this, adding that they were careful to throw their trash a considerable distance away from the city walls.

550 (d) 6 Jumādā'l-Awwal, 981: A Muslim was accused of having let his wife and daughter traffic with strangers. Khaḍr the Damascene Jew was mentioned as one of those who actually had a hidden passage dug to enable them to enter his adjacent abode unnoticed.

562 (d) 21 Jumādā'l-Awwal, 981: A Jewish rabbi from Safed died during his pilgrimage to Hebron. His wife (names provided) was declared as the person entitled to inherit all his belongings in spite of attempts to have them confiscated by the official in charge of the "treasury" of heirless deceased people (*amīn bayt al-māl*).

593 (b) 1 Rajab, 981: Yūsif b. Sālim the Jew was accused of keeping wine in his shop in the Jewish quarter. When the court sent a group of Muslims there to investigate the case, he was found guilty of public display of wine in spite of earlier warnings. Thereupon the kadi ruled that the Jew be punished accordingly.

612 (a) 7 Sha'bān, 981: The head of the Jewish community, Shamīla b. Abū Jūkār, leased the income due to the endowment of the Temple Mount for inheritances of heirless Jews (referred to as "the Jewish treasury"–*bayt māl al-yahūd*) for the annual sum of twelve and a half

sulṭānī gold coins, an increase of 20 percent over the sum pledged for the previous year.

622 (b) 19 Sha'bān, 981: The head of the Jewish community delivered the poll tax due from his community for the year 981 A.H. to the authorities.

631 (a) 17 Jumādā'l-'Ūlā, 981: The Muslim supply officer (*jebejī*) of the Citadel sold his right to a daily salary of 6 silver coins to the Jew Ya'qūb b. Ibrāhīm, who paid him 25 *sulṭānī* gold coins for it. This transaction was sanctioned in court by the commanding officer (*dizdār*) of the Citadel. (For other references see also *sijill* 55/631 (b-c) and 639 (a)).

Volume 56
(1574 - 1576)

23 (h) 3 Shawwāl, 981: Maryam b. Ismā'īl, a Jewish woman, complained in court that her room was broken into during the day while she was visiting a neighbor, and several of her belongings (a list provided) were stolen. The Muslim she accused of having been seen nearby when she returned, denied all knowledge of the case.

59 (d) 19 Dhū'l-Qa'da, 981: Mūsā b. Abū Jūkār reported in court that after he had left his home to go to his shop at the Jewish small market (*sūwayqa*), his mother too went away to bake bread at the bakery (*furn*) while his wife took their child to school (*kuttāb*). Upon her return his wife discovered that their house had been broken into and several pieces of jewelry (a detailed list provided) stolen.

61 (g) 23 Dhū'l-Qa'da, 981: The Jewish cloth merchant Khaḍr b. Aṣlān gave power of attorney to a former Jerusalem Jew now living in Damascus, to annul by mutual consent (*mufāsakha*) an earlier agreement with a Muslim merchant for the sale of a substantial consignment of soap (about 48 *qinṭār* for 900 gold coins). The soap had been stored in the soap factory by another agent of his, the Jerusalem spice dealer (*'aṭṭār*) Yūsif b. 'Abd al-Karīm.

61 (h) 23 Dhū'l-Qa'da, 981: The Muslim merchant declares in court that he absolves the Jewish partner in the above-mentioned soap deal from all responsibility and fully agrees to the rescinding of the earlier business arrangement.

61 (i) 23 Dhū'l-Qa'da, 981: The deputy commander (*katkhudā*) of the Citadel in his capacity, inter alia, as administrator (*mutawallī*), of the Ṭūrghūd pasha endowment, agreed to receive the above-mentioned soap consignment as a deposit of the newly assigned Jewish agent.

122 (c) 2 Ṣafar, 982: A Jew from Safed was commissioned by another Jew who had leased "the new bathhouse" (*al-ḥammām al-jadīd*) of Safed, to deliver the sum of 4320 silver coins to the reciters (*qurrā'*) of Koran verses at The Dome of the Rock.

123 (f) 4 Ṣafar, 982: A group of 191 Jewish pilgrims from North Africa to Jerusalem tried to avoid payment of the road tax (*khafar*) at Funduqūmiyya village and in Nablus on the pretext that the term "infidels" (*kafara*) did not apply to them. The kadi sought a legal opinion from the Hanafite *muftī* of Jerusalem who ruled that they do fall within this category, hence they are liable to the tax.

130 (f) 13 Ṣafar, 982: The Hanafite *muftī* of Jerusalem acknowledged receipt of the annual poll tax due from the Jewish community as part of his salary (*mawājib*) for that year. His statement was confirmed by the heads of the community (names provided).

199 (a) 24 Jumādā'l-Awwal, 982: The sister of Salamūn Shulāl was the owner of a house in the Jewish quarter. At an earlier date she had requested the kadi's permission to repair several parts, and once this was granted, she had the house repaired. When rumors reached the court to the effect that she did not abide by the specific stipulation ruling that no new elements should be added, an inspection committee was sent there. It presented the court with a detailed description of the substantial and luxurious unauthorized changes made in the building (details provided).

201 (c) 21 Jumādā'l-Awwal, 982: Shamīla, the head of the Jewish community, sued one Jew, then another, for the gold coin he paid for each of them on account of their poll tax.

211 (b) 5 Jumādā'l-Thānī, 982: The kadi ruled that a certain member of the Jewish community repay Shamīla, the head of the community for his outstanding poll tax.

211 (c) 5 Jumādā'l-Thānī, 982: Estīr b. Yahūdā, the mother of Simḥa b. Aṣlān who was referred to in *sijill*, p. 199 (a)

above, described in great detail the repairs that her daughter made in her house. "Since it was in her possession (*mulk*)" she asked for the kadi's authorization retroactively for the several new elements added to the building. Her request was duly granted.

243 (f) 26 Rajab, 982: The *sūbāshī* of Jerusalem issued a formal warning to both Christians and Jews that they should not sell any wine to the Muslims.

243 (g) 26 Rajab, 982: The Jew Shmū'īl b. Hārūn and his Muslim partner owe the orphans of another Muslim 29 gold coins for 35 sheep entrusted to them by the orphans' deceased father.

251 (f) 29 Rajab, 982: A Muslim merchant accused the Jewess Simḥa b. Aṣlān of having stolen two very special tiles from his house. When two witnesses attested to the validity of his argument she was instructed by the court to return them, and she complied.

257 (b) 16 Sha'bān, 982: A Muslim accused the heads of the Jewish community of owing his brother 100 gold coins and demanded that they pay him half of this sum. They admitted their debt but refused to pay him as long as he could not produce any binding authorization from his brother. The kadi ruled in their favor.

278 (a) 6 Ramaḍān, 982: A Jew was apprehended by the night watchers patrolling the town with the *sūbāshī* after "the beating of the drums" that announced the regular night curfew. He excused himself by submitting that he had been visiting with friends and was on his way home, but the kadi ruled that he should be punished.

283 (d) 13 Shawwāl, 982: The Jewess Ḥannā b. Yahūdā requested the court's approval to collect a debt of 10 gold coins she had paid for her deceased son-in-law, Ya'qūb, from the inheritance of his two minor daughters and son. Both her daughter and her grandson confirmed her allegation, hence her request was granted by the kadi.

288 (d) 11 Shawwāl, 982: 'Aṭiyya b. Ya'qūb, the above-mentioned Jewish grandson, accused his

grandmother Ḥannā of having taken unjustified possession of a long list of items left by his deceased father, including 100 gold coins' worth of Egyptian cloth.

290 (e) 13 Shawwāl, 982: A detailed list of all of the belongings of the deceased Jew Ya'qūb b. 'Aṭiyya, to be inherited by his wife, son and daughters. His Jewish mother-in-law appointed a Muslim agent to sell some of the items mortgaged with her out of this inheritance in return for a debt her son-in-law had owed her.

393 (g) 25 Rabī' al-Awwal, 983: A detailed description of several houses owned by Muslims and located "at the gate of the Jewish quarter (*bāb ḥārat al-yahūd*)".

400 (d) 10 Rabī' al-Thānī, 983: The *muḥtasib* in charge of inspection in the markets accused the Jew Yahūdā b. 'Abd al-Karīm of the unlawful use of the recently abolished copper and other defective coins. The specific order declared all copper and lead coins as void and out of circulation, to be replaced by properly stamped (*makhtūma*) "red and black" *fulūs* coins. For a summary of the original order, including the exchange rate of the newly introduced coins, see *sijill*, p. 393 (f).

416 (d) The first third of Jumādā'l-'Ūlā, 983: The officials in charge of collecting the poll tax due for the year 983 from the various districts of Palestine acknowledged receipt from Shamīla, the head of the community, of the entire sum due from the Jewish community of Jerusalem. Part of it had already been paid to the *muftī* of Jerusalem as per an earlier order sent from Istanbul.

418 (i) 28 Rabī' al-Thānī, 983: A Muslim accused the Jewess Simḥa b. Isḥāq, in the presence of her brother-in-law, of having been living unlawfully in the house called *dār al-fustuqa* located at the gate of the Jewish quarter which was part of a Muslim endowment of which he was comptroller (*nāẓir*). She confirmed the facts adding that she had been regularly paying her rent for it to the administrator (*mutawallī*) of the endowment who also gave her receipts accordingly.

419 (c) 14 Rabīʻ al-Thānī, 983: The Jew Yahūdā b. ʻAbd al-Karīm bought from the Jew Mūsā b. Nasīm an apartment (*ṭabaqa)* on the upper floor of a house at al-Rīsha quarter, bordering on other Jewish houses. The seller confirmed the transaction and full payment as well as the additional rights accruing to the buyer (i.e. use of the cistern to draw water, or that of the kitchen [*murtafaq*] located in the building).

435 (c) 21 Jumādā'l-'Ūlā, 983: The Jew Yaʻqūb b. Shāsh was accused by the Jew Ibrāhīm b. Yūsif of drinking wine in public as well as conducting himself in an aggressive manner towards his fellow Jews. When the defendant confessed to all these accusations he was sentenced to be flogged (*taʻzīr*).

465 (d) 11 Rajab, 983: A certain Jewish cloth merchant from Safed was authorized by the comptroller (*nāẓir)* of the endowment of al-Aqṣā Mosque to collect the poll tax they owed this year for the endowment from the Christians of the Safed district.

495 (e) 17 Ramaḍān, 983: Another Jewish cloth merchant from Safed was personally involved in the collection of income due to the endowment of the Tombs of the Patriarchs in Hebron as well as that of al-Aqṣā Mosque in Jerusalem. Document ends on p. 496 (a).

501 (b) The second third of Ramaḍān, 983: Two distinguished Jewish leaders attest to the validity of a marriage concluded between two members of their community (names provided) as well as to the financial arrangements involved.

535 (a) 29 Dhū'l-Qaʻda, 983: Several distinguished members of the Jewish community (eight names provided) complained of the behavior of a member of their community who drinks wine in public and even offers it to Muslims in flagrant violation of local tradition. The Jew in question was summoned to court, formally warned by the kadi against any further behavior of this kind, then vowed to refrain from similar acts in the future and pledged to pay a substantial fine if he broke his promise.

545 (f) 1 Dhū'l-Qa'da, 983: The kadi authorized Bārūkh b. Salamūn, the Jewish trustee (*waṣiy)* of the Jewish minor, Sāsūn b. Mūsā b. Ṣūfān, to spend one silver coin every day on the various vital expenses (*nafaqa*) of the child.

555 (d) 1 Muḥarram, 984: The Jewish cloth merchant Yūsif b. Sha'bān accused Khudāwirdī, the former *sūbāshī* of Nablus, of not honoring a debt he owed him for a mantle (*burnus)* he had sold him. Khudāwirdī acknowledged the debt but claimed that he had it debited to another Muslim. When the latter allegation was confirmed by two Muslim witnesses Khudāwirdī was released from jail.

585 (e) 27 Muḥarram, 984: The Jewish money changer (*ṣayrafī*) at the governor's court (*dīwān)* in Cairo, Nātān b. Shmū'īl Kūhān b. Shams, sold his Corsican slave for the sum of 50 gold coins to an Egyptian Copt. Most of this price was actually paid by the Jewish sesame oil dealer (*sayrajānī)* and the rest was spent on oil for the illumination of the Tombs of the Patriarchs in Hebron.

597 (a) 25 Shawwāl, 983: The Jewish cloth merchant, Mā'īr b. Ibrāhīm, was appointed by the official in charge of the endowments of the Temple Mount in Jerusalem and the Tombs of the Patriarchs in Hebron, to collect the poll tax due to these endowments for the year 984. A long list of Christian names of inhabitants of several towns and villages in Palestine is provided.

618 (b) 22 Rajab, 983: The governor of Jerusalem owed the Safed Jewish cloth merchant, Mā'īr b. Ibrāhīm, the very substantial amount of 550 *sulṭānī* gold coins for a consignment of colored *jawkh* broad cloth as well as Safed cushions (*maqā'id*). This old debt has now been paid, partly in cash, and mostly in kind (wheat, barley and bitumen, quantities and prices provided).

618 (c) 22 Rajab, 983: The same governor of Jerusalem paid another Safed Jew, Isḥāq b. Lawī, an old debt of 338 gold coins for a variety of colored pieces of cloth (Safed, *isqalāṭ*). The debt was paid partly in cash, but mostly in kind (barley, rice, bitumen).

Volume 57
(1576 - 1577)

13 (g) 14 Rabīʿ al-Awwal, 984: A Muslim camel-driver had been hired by the Egyptian Jew Nātān b. Shmūʾīl, the money changer at the court (*dīwān*) of the governor of Cairo, to take him to Jerusalem. He was promised the sum of 12 gold coins; the last portion of that sum has now been paid, at the end of his four month contract.

25 (a) The last third of Rabīʿ al-Awwal, 984: The high-ranking official who arrived from Damascus in order to levy the poll tax from the non-Muslims of Jerusalem, commissioned the head of the Jewish community, Shamīla, with the collection of the tax due from the Jews. Part of the dues of the 60 tax tickets of this tax was discounted as it had already been credited to the Hanafite *muftī* of the town.

31 (g) 3 Rabīʿ al-Thānī, 984: The heads of the Jewish community (names provided) asked for the court's help to stop their ongoing harassment by a certain Muslim. This person (whose name–Dālī ʿAlī–indicates eccentricity and a possible *Ṣūfī* connection) was summoned to the court where he was formally warned against any infringement on their synagogue and against appearing in its vicinity at any time, failing which he will be severely flogged and imprisoned for a long period.

90 (c) 18 Jumādā'l Thānī, 984: The Jew Yahūdā b. Saʿīd failed to pay his debt to his Christian creditor. When the delay he was granted expired he gave his creditor a mule he owned and was compensated for the difference by a cash payment of 2 gold and 10 silver coins.

139 (e) 23 Shaʿbān, 984: A Muslim woman appointed her husband as her agent in her law-suit against the Jewess Malīḥa b. Mūsā whom she accused of unlawfully keeping in her possession a pair of her earrings.

139 (f) 23 Sha'bān, 984: The above-mentioned case involved a pair of "pear" shaped (*injāṣ*) earrings set with precious stones and pearls that were allegedly mortgaged against a loan of 3 gold coins.

139 (g) 23 Sha'bān, 984: A Muslim woman from the village of al-Bīra accused the widow of a Jewish silversmith of a debt incurred by her deceased husband who allegedly did not provide the Muslim with bracelets she had commissioned from him. When adequate testimony was given in court the kadi ruled that the debt be paid from the widow's inheritance.

265 (b) 5 Muḥarram, 985: The head of the surgeons' guild (*jarrāḥiyya*) warned the Jew Shiḥāda b. Ibrāhīm to refrain from the practice of any medical operation (*faṣl wa-takḥīl*) until he masters all aspects of this profession.

340 (b) 27 Rabī' al-Awwal, 985: The head of the Jewish community, Shamīla, delivered to the high-ranking official in charge of the collection of the poll tax, the sums that are due from the community for the year 985. He was acquitted of part of this sum on account of earlier payments made to the Hanafite *muftī* of Jerusalem for his salary.

344 (i) 3 Rabī' al-Thānī, 985: A Muslim sued the Jewish cobbler, Ya'qūb b. 'Āzir, for a debt he owed for three camel-hides he had sold him for four and a half gold coins.

349 (f) 9 Rabī' al-Thānī, 985: The Jew Yahūdā b. Ibrāhīm rented a house in the Jewish quarter that was part of a Muslim endowment. He was authorized by the comptroller (*nāẓir*) to spend parts of his rent on reconstruction of several parts of the building. An account is provided detailing the various sums spent in the course of several years on the repairs, all of which are validated by the comptroller.

386 (f) 13 Jumādā'l-'Ūlā, 985: Several Muslim dyers (*ṣabbāgh*) acknowledged their debt to the Jerusalem Jewish cloth merchant, Mā'īr b. Ibrāhīm, for consignments (weights and prices provided) of indigo from the Jordan rift (*nīl ghawrī*) which he had sold them. Both parties agree to

defer payment of the entire sum of 115 gold coins for a period of four months.

485 (c) 25 Rajab, 985: An official investigation was initiated by the kadi upon the request of the *sūbāshī* in charge of law and order in Jerusalem into the sudden death of a Jewish woman, Qamar b. Mūsā, who had gone to bathe at ‘Ayn Silwān fountain. The kadi sent a special envoy to investigate the matter, and the latter had two Muslim women inspect her body thoroughly. No traces of any violence were found on the body. Qamar's nephew reported to the judge that he had escorted her together with two other Jews to the fountainhead at the request of her husband, Yahūdā the rabbi (*al-dayyān*), after an extended illness she had suffered, and her death was sudden and unprovoked.

488 (b) 12 Jumādā'l Thānī, 985: Yahūdā b. Saʿīd testified that after several days he had spent with his brother-in-law Shmū'īl b. Sāsī in the village of ‘Ajlūl, the latter decided to return to Jerusalem. He sent him back accompanied by two donkeys loaded with wheat, but some time later his body was found in the vicinity of the village. The court sent an investigation committee to the village to inspect the body on which was found clear evidence of murder.

Volume 58
(1578 - 1579)

83 (a) 22 Muḥarram, 986: Two distinguished Muslim merchants sold a house they owned in partnership to the Jewish "master"(*mu'allim)* Yahūdā b. Yūsif. They had bought it from a Jewish owner (Qamar b. Ibrāhīm) in 978 and sold it now for the substantial price of 120 gold coins. The house is located in al-Sharaf quarter (formerly known as al-Ṣalātīn, also as Ibn 'Unatāt quarter) it consists of two storys and borders on Jewish and non-Jewish properties (details provided).

122 (c) 7 Rabī' al-Awwal, 986: The Jew Ya'qūb b. Yūsif declared in court that from now on he would not contradict his father and will involve himself deeply in the study of reading and writing. The father undertook to marry him to a Jewish woman from Safed since he formally declared himself unattached to a certain other Jewish woman.

157 (g) 21 Rabī' al-Thānī, 986: The Jewish spice dealer Yūsif b. 'Abd al-Karīm lent his son Ya'qūb 40 gold coins. The son undertook to obey his father in every way, as well as to dedicate himself to his reading lessons. The kadi validated their mutual agreement.

188 (f) 28 Jumādā'l-Awwal, 986: The Jewish physician "master" Yūsif b. "master" Ibrāhīm bought a dilapidated two story building owned by a Muslim in the Jewish quarter, for the sum of 29 gold coins. The building bordered on several other Jewish properties, including "the Jewish hospital (*bīmāristān*)" and another house owned by the same buyer.

235 (f) 17 Shawwāl, 986: Ya'qūb b. Yūsif b. 'Abd al-Karīm declared in court that that very day he divorced his wife Sāra b. Ibrāhīm from Safed who was identified by two Jewish witnesses. Both parties, i.e. Ya'qūb and his father on the one hand, and Sāra and her mother on the

other hand, absolved one another from any obligation or debt whatsoever.

253 (f) 9 Dhū'l-Qa'da, 986: The above-mentioned Ya'qūb b. Yūsif alleged in court that another Jew, Shmū'īl b. Khalīfa, had promised him his minor daughter, Mazalṭūf, in marriage for 25 gold coins as bride-money. Shmū'īl denied it and referred the court to an earlier deposition by the same plaintiff (see above, *sijill* 58/122 (c)) in which Ya'qūb specifically referred to his daughter as totally unrelated to him.

268 (c) The last third of Dhū'l-Qa'da, 986: Several distinguished members of the Jewish community (names provided) were accused in court by the *sūbāshī* of Jerusalem of wearing Muslim garb in their synagogues, thereby defying specific orders ruling against it. They produced a legal opinion (*fatwā*) of the highest religious authority, Abū'l Su'ūd Efendī from Istanbul, as well as imperial orders based upon it, authorizing the Jewish custom "from time immemorial" of wearing their most elegant clothes in the synagogue as well as covering their heads with prayer shawls (*ṭaylasān*) made of white cloth or wool while they conduct their prayers. The kadi adopted all these documents and ruled accordingly against any attempt to interfere with these Jewish customs.

289 (a) 4 Dhū'l-Ḥijja, 986: A Muslim sued the Jewish spice dealer Ya'qūb b. Yūsif b. 'Abd al-Karīm for not paying for spices, silk and various receptacles he had sold him. The defendant denied the allegation but when two valid witnesses were presented he was forced to pay.

289 (c) 17 Dhū'l-Ḥijja, 986: Yahūdā b. 'Abd al-Karīm sued his nephew Ya'qūb for having sold him the last part of his merchandise from the very shop he had sold earlier on. The kadi imposed full payment on the nephew.

289 (g) 5 Dhū'l-Ḥijja, 986: The Jew Yahūdā b. Sa'īd sued a Muslim woman who allegedly bought from his late mother two cotton garments (*quṭayna*) which he now demanded in his capacity as her sole heir. The defendant denied the allegation and even agreed to give

a solemn oath in court that she had no knowledge of the garments.

299 (d) 29 Dhū'l-Ḥijja, 986: An imperial order was brought to Jerusalem by the Jewish tax collector (*'āmil)* Nāthān b. "master" Shmū'īl from Egypt. It permitted the reconstruction and renovation of old, dilapidated buildings they owned in town. The kadi inspected the evidence, then ruled to grant the Jews their request and to refrain from any attempt to stand in their way.

300 (a) 28 Dhū'l-Ḥijja, 986: The Jew Yūsif b. Ibrāhīm, representing his brother Nātān who was in charge of the Ashkenazi Jewish hospital, requested the court's permission to repair the hospital building which had reached a lamentable state. The kadi granted permission to conduct wide-scale repairs, both in- and outside the building.

353 (b) 17 Ṣafar, 987: Although no wheat may be sold in Jerusalem outside of "the lot of the grains" (*'arṣat al-ghilāl)*, two Jewish brothers admitted having violated this regulation. They were standing in front of their house in the Jewish quarter (*maḥalla*) near "the old gate of the Jewish quarter (*ḥāra*)" when a Muslim from the village Qalūnyā came by carrying three loads of wheat. They bought his merchandise, disregarding the above restriction. The kadi ruled that they be severely punished.

404 (f) 11 Rabī' al-Thānī, 987: A list of authorized butchers includes two Jewish names: The "master" (*al-mu'allim*) 'Aṭūn the butcher and Mūsā the Jewish meat-seller (*bayyā')*.

404 (g) 11 Rabī' al-Thānī, 987: The Jewish merchant *khawāja* Ibrāhīm b. Mūsā rented a house in the Jewish quarter from a Muslim merchant for an annual rental of two and a half gold coins.

410 (c) 17 Rabī' al-Thānī, 987: The Egyptian Jew, "master" (*mu'allim)* Dā'ūd b. Ya'qūb accused the Jerusalemite Jew Mūsā b. Abū Jūkār of a debt of 200 gold coins he had given him for the purchase of soap. The defendant denied it, but the plaintiff summoned two valid Jewish

witnesses who confirmed that they had heard the accused acknowledge this debt publicly.

415 (a) 20 Rabīʿ al-Thānī, 987: A Muslim merchant in Jerusalem was commissioned by an Egyptian Jew to buy him a consignment of olive oil and have it "cooked" in Jerusalem in the traditionally proper way to produce soap. The substantial amount of 587 gold coins given to him would be used in this transaction as a form of limited partnership (*muḍāraba*) between the two men. Details (prices, weights etc.) of the actual deal are cited, the oil was bought and stored in a soap factory, and ways were agreed upon as to how the soap, once made, would be sent to Egypt.

415 (c) 22 Rabīʿ al-Thānī, 987: Yūsif b. Yahūdā the Jew, the brother-in-law of the Jewish money changer in the court (*dīwān*) of the governor of Cairo, "master" Shmū'īl the Cohen (*al-kūhān*), paid a Muslim in Jerusalem the sum of 50 gold coins owed him by the heads of the Jewish community of Jerusalem (10 names provided). This sum was actually sent by "master" Shmū'īl for the payment of this debt.

415 (d) 22 Rabīʿ al-Thānī, 987: The above-mentioned Yūsif paid another Muslim another debt owed him by the heads of the Jerusalem community, this time 33 gold coins, also sent by the Cairene Jewish money changer, "master" Shmū'īl.

444 (c) 25 Rabīʿ al-Thānī, 987: Marḥaba b. Yūsif, the wife of an Egyptian Jew, reported to the court when summoned to do so that she had purchased her maid in Cairo two years before as an infidel (*kāfira*) for the sum of 60 gold coins. The maid declared herself to be Muslim and formerly in the service of a Muslim master. Thereupon she was taken away from her Jewish mistress and put in the custody of the commander of the Citadel.

444 (d) 25 Rabīʿ al-Thānī, 987: A group of Egyptian Jewish pilgrims headed by ʿAṭiyya b. Shmū'āl the Cohen (*al-kūhān*) arrived in Jerusalem allegedly to visit it as well as Hebron, but actually as refugees fleeing the plague. When they were not permitted to enter Jerusalem they produced a letter of recommendation

from the governor of Cairo, and were then permitted to come in as pilgrims. Their extended stay caused a variety of protests of the Muslims of the town who complained of their unusually arrogant behavior, their wearing of Muslim clothing, employment of Muslim maids and causing scarcity of food and a general rise in prices. Several attempts by the local authorities to convince those Jews to leave and return home proved futile, until a plague broke out in Jerusalem, too, whereupon all of them left.

533 (b) The first third of Ṣafar, 987: Another copy (unfinished, with several modifications) of *sijill* 58/444 (d) above.

536 (b) 25 Rabīʿ al-Thānī, 987: Another copy of *sijill* 58/444 (d).

541 (b) 8 Ṣafar, 987: The Jerusalem Jewish cloth merchant, *khawāja* Māʾīr b. Ibrāhīm, paid the debt of 185 gold coins he owed the kadi of Jerusalem for two pieces of cloth (3 *dhirāʿ* of one kind, and 5 *dhirāʿ* of another) he had allegedly given him.

565 (c) 14 Jumādā'l-Awwal, 986: The head of the community, Shamīla, reported in court that a Jewish blind man, Saʿīd b. Sulaymān, while walking in the Jewish neighborhood (*maḥalla*) fell into a cave ("the cave of the grinding-mill") and a day later died. A special committee sent to his home presented the court with a detailed report on the state of the body.

571 (c) 16 Rabīʿ al-Thānī, 986: A group of Shāfiʿī butchers complained to the kadi of the Jewish slaughtering: since the Jews insert their hands into the animal's body in order to verify whether it is *qūshīr* or *'iṭreyf*, it should be declared forbidden to Muslims. When the kadi asked the heads of the community about it, they presented two separate legal opinions of the chief *muftī* of Istanbul, the authoritative Abū'l Suʿūd, declaring Jewish slaughtering admissible in spite of their introducing their hands into the animal's body. They also presented the court with an imperial order issued in the year 975 instructing that the above legal opinions should be acted upon. Thereupon the kadi authorized the Jewish slaughtering once again.

Volume 59
(1580 - 1581)

44 (b) 19 Dhū'l-Ḥijja, 987: Yahūdā b. Mūsā "the blacksmith" (*al-ḥaddād*), Yūsif b. Sha'bān, Shamīla "the head of the Jews" (*shaykh al-yahūd),* Isḥāq b. Ibrāhīm, Ibrāhīm b. Isḥāq–all of these members of the Jewish community–accused a certain Muslim of an attempt to steal several lamps from their synagogue. He denied their claim as well as that accusing him of hitting another Jew and pulling his beard. In view of their lack of any corroborating evidence and the defendant's oath that he had done nothing of this sort, he was not reprimanded, but was very specifically warned against any similar behavior in the future.

87 (a) 17 Muḥarram, 988: A group of distinguished Shāfi'ī people submitted to the kadi a complaint very similar to the one described in volume 58, p. 571 (c). Their request was that he stop the Jews from slaughtering, but several Jewish leaders not only described to the court the background justifying their slaughtering, but also quoted the ruling of the kadi on this matter dating from more than a year and a half earlier. Thereupon the kadi reconfirmed the former decision and authorized their slaughtering.

93 (e) 23 Ṣafar, 988: A group of Jews reported to the kadi a robbery that occurred the night before in their synagogue: *Khawāja* Mā'īr b. Ibrāhīm, Yūsif b. Sha'bān, Yahūdā b. Yada', Yahūdā b. Mūsā the blacksmith (*al-ḥaddād*), Yahūdā b. 'Abd al-Karīm, his brother Yūsif, Salamūn b. Mūsā Shulāl, Shamīla b. *al-sayrajānī,* Yahūdā the Ashkenazi (*al-amanī*), and Ibrāhīm the beadle (*khādim kanīsatihim*). The detailed list of items stolen included many rugs, embroided curtains of the ark, Torah (*sifr al-tūrāh)* coverings, Torah silver crowns and plates, silver pointers etc. The *sūbāshī* of Jerusalem undertook the investigation of the matter.

95 (k) 28 Dhū'l-Ḥijja, 987: Shmīla b. *al-sayrajānī* ("the sesame oil dealer") applied for the kadi's permission to collect the poll tax of the Jews for the year 988 in order to give it to the agent of the comptroller of the endowments of the Temple Mount and the Tombs of the Patriarchs. His request was granted.

167 (f) 18 Jumādā'l-Thānī, 988: *Khawāja* Mā'īr, b. Ibrāhīm reported to the court the poor state of many houses that belonged to members of the Jewish community. He presented the court with an earlier imperial order issued toward the end of 984 authorizing the reconstruction of their dilapidated buildings in the Jewish neighborhood of Jerusalem. Thereupon the kadi issued a permit to the Jews authorizing repairs and reconstruction of all sorts to their buildings.

168 (a) 17 Jumādā'l-Thānī, 988: A general order had been issued to verify the exact number of Jews liable to poll tax in the province of Damascus. The dignitaries (*a'yān*) of the Jewish community, *khawāja* Mā'īr, Yahūdā b. Mūsā the blacksmith and Yūsif b. 'Abd al-Karīm, were summoned to the court to hear this order read. The official in charge of the inspection carried out a public as well as a secret search, and found no changes in the numbers or names recorded in earlier existing official statistical documents.

260 (b) 22 Dhū'l-Qa'da, 988: The Jew Shmū'īl b. Faraj-Allah sold the Jewish cloth merchant *khawāja* Yūsif b. Sha'bān, both of them residents of Jerusalem, a house in al-Sharaf quarter (*ḥārat al-ḥayādira min maḥallat al-sharaf)* for 130 gold coins. On all sides the house borders on buildings owned by Muslims (among them a janissary officer).

351 (a) 7 Rabī' al-Awwal, 989: The Jewess Nabīla b. Mināḥim accused a Muslim builder of having stolen several pieces of jewelry (details provided) from her room when she went to the synagogue during the Passover. Although it was located in the house of Shiḥāda, the Jewish oculist (*kaḥḥāl*), she locked it before leaving, and when she returned the lock was broken open and the jewelry missing. The builder explained that having seen that some of the Jews "were buying and selling" he

thought it was not a holiday after all, and he could come to work on the assignment given to him earlier by the owner of the house. When he entered the house he saw that there was nobody present, so he left. He first denied her accusation, then agreed to pay her 4 gold coins in order to settle the matter finally. She accepted.

558 (d) 19 Jumādā'l-Thānī, 989: The comptroller (*nāẓir)* of the endowment of the Temple Mount and the Tombs of the Patriarchs accused the head of the Jewish community, Shamīla b. Yūsif the sesame oil dealer (*al-sayrajānī*), of having unlawfully taken possession of all income accruing from "the Jewish Treasury" which actually belonged to The Dome of the Rock endowment. Since the annual rate of this lease was 50 gold coins, it was alleged that he owed 500 for the past ten years. He denied this claim and the plaintiff was asked to present his evidence.

Volume 61
(1582 - 1583)

11 (c) 21 Muḥarram, 990: The kadi appointed a head of the silversmiths' guild at the suggestion of the Christian and Jewish silversmiths (names provided).

119 (b) 14 Rabīʻ al-Awwal, 990: An inventory (over 100 items) of the belongings of the deceased Jew Salamūn b. Yahūdā b. Mūsā Shulāl.

148 (b) 20 Rabīʻ al-Thānī, 990: The Jew Shamīla b. Mūsā accused the Jew Ya'qūb b. Yūsif of having caused him to be fined by the *ṣūbashī*. Yaʻqūb was prohibited by the kadi from further entering the premises of the *ṣūbashī*.

226 (d) 1 Rajab, 990: The court was asked by the Jew Shūbā b. Dā'ūd to force his wife Sulṭāna b. Ibrāhīm to return to his home. She admitted living with her brother and explained that she left her husband's house when he took another Jewish wife.

227 (b) 1 Rajab, 990: The above-mentioned woman accused her above-mentioned husband of practicing sodomy on her. The husband denied the allegation.

284 (e) End of Rajab, 990: The Jew Sāsī b. Faraj-Allah was accused by a shoe-maker of having ordered shoes to be manufactured for him out of water buffalo hides. He claimed to have taken 260 pairs but upon the shoe-maker's request they were counted and found to be actually 276 pairs.

357 (g) 9 Dhū'l-Qaʻda, 990: The Jew Yahūdā b. ʻAbd al-Karīm was appointed by the kadi as head of the Jewish community of Jerusalem upon the recommendation of the Jews Yūsif b. ʻAbd al-Karīm and Yūsif b. Shaʻbān.

506 (f) 3 Muḥarram, 991: Upon the request of the head of the Jewish community, Dā'ūd, a clear warning was issued

by the kadi to the Jewish butcher Mūsā b. Shmū'īl to refrain from all slaughtering of sheep.

Volume 62
(1583 - 1584)

30 (d) 13 Jumādā'l-Awwal, 991: The Jewish cloth merchant (*jawkhī*) *al-khawāja* Mā'īr b. Ibrāhīm owed 162 gold coins to a Muslim *sipāhī* officer. So far the debtor had paid the equivalent of 15 gold coins by delivering 30 *mudd* of wheat. The rest, as promised by the Jew, will be paid in two months' time.

53 (b) 27 Jumādā'l-Awwal, 991: The Jew Dā'ūd had been the tax collector (*'āmil*) in Bāb al-Naṣr in Cairo and in this capacity was in charge of collecting taxes due from soap import. Six Muslim merchants from Jerusalem claimed to have paid him when their soap loads came into Cairo. The kadi did not agree to exempt them from paying again because Dā'ūd's tenure had been terminated two years before when it became known that he had embezzled the funds levied.

59 (d) 23 Jumādā'l-'Ūlā, 991: The Jews Mā'īr b. Ibrāhīm and Dā'ūd b. Yahūdā delivered to the officer, sent by the high official in charge of finances (*defterdār*) of Damascus, all the poll tax due from the Jewish community for 60 people.

260 (d) 7 Shawwāl, 991: The head of the Jewish community Yūsif b. Sha'bān requested permission to set up a bakery for the Jews in a house located in their quarter near their market. Permission was granted.

260 (e) 7 Shawwāl, 991: The Jew Yūsif b. Sha'bān requested permission to rebuild a room that deteriorated as a result of the heavy rains. Permission was granted upon inspection.

301 (h) 8 Ramaḍān, 991: The kadi ordered Ya'qūb (?) b. Yūsif to leave the house of his father in the Jewish quarter because of his recurrent disobedience.

343 (c) [No date mentioned.] The Jew Shmū'īl b. Shiḥāda accused the Jewish woman Manūḥa b. Mūsā of having cursed him in public. When she denied it, two Jewish witnesses confirmed his claim. The woman was found guilty and flogged.

403 (d) 2 Muḥarram, 992: A dispute between a Jewish merchant from Damascus and several mule-drivers whom he hired for the transport of his goods between Jerusalem and Damascus.

406 (i) 16 Muḥarram, 992: *Al-khawāja* Mā'īr b. Ibrāhīm and Sāsī b. Shmū'īl, the heads of the Jewish community, paid the poll tax due from their community to the endowment of the Temple Mount. The total figure was 85 people, 50 silver coins per head.

Volume 64
(1584 - 1585)

85 (b) 12 Sha'bān, 992: The Jew Khalīl b. Shiḥāda accused the Jew Ibrāhīm b. Ya'qūb of having attacked him and having plucked hair from his beard. The accusation was confirmed by two Jewish witnesses (names provided).

125 (f) 19 Ramaḍān, 992: The Jew Mūsā b. Yahūdā accused 3 Jews (names provided) of having attacked and beaten him in the synagogue.

131 (a) 13 Shawwāl, 992: A large house that had been endowed to the Karaite community was taken over by several *ṣūbāshīs* and vacated only after the alleged payment of 6 gold coins. Then 7 additional gold coins were spent on repairs and reconstruction. The Karaite who claimed to have spent all these sums was then approached by another Karaite who claimed that this was his family's property, and that when his father endowed it he specified that if any of his descendants lived in Jerusalem they would be entitled to use it. When sufficient evidence was brought, the kadi ruled that the defendant use the house pending payment of all the expenses of the plaintiff for the actual repairs.

184 (f) 22 Dhū'l-Ḥijja, 922: A financial dispute between a Christian and the Jew Shmū'īl b. Khalīfa.

185 (a) 15 Dhū'l-Ḥijja, 922: The Moroccan *mu'allim* Ya'qūb b. Raḥamīm purchased from the Jewish cloth merchant *khawāja* Yūsif b. Sha'bān b. Ibrāhīm a house "in al-Ḥayādira neighborhood (*ḥāra)* in al-Sharaf quarter (*maḥalla*)" with a mulberry tree, vines, roses and vegetables, bordering on other houses owned by Muslims, for the sum of 250 gold coins.

248 9 Rabī' al-Awwal, 993: A very detailed description of the dispute between Muslims and Jews as to the origins

of, and the right to worship in, the Nahmanides Synagogue.

252 (a) 20 Rabīʻ al-Awwal, 993: A Muslim from al-Walaja village sold an orchard in that village for 12 gold coins to the Jew Dā'ūd b. Yahūdā b. ʻAbd al-Karīm, head of the Jewish community.

266 (c) 21 Rabīʻ al-Awwal, 993: The kadi, upon a request of the head of the guild, warned 5 Jewish silversmiths (names provided) to buy all the silver and gold they need only from qualified people.

277 (b) 3 Rabīʻ al-Thānī, 923: An imperial decree forbids the Jews from wearing a headgear (*ʻamāma*) resembling that of the Muslims.

288 (h) 9 Ṣafar, 993: Barakat b. Abraham the Karaite owed Sulaymān b. ʻAbd al-ʻĀl the Karaite a few items.

318 (d) 13 Rabīʻ al-Awwal, 993: The kadi demanded that the Jews Yūsif b. ʻAbd al-Karīm and Yahūdā b. *al-ḥaddād* bring the document concerning their synagogue.

340 (b) 10 Jumādā'l-'Ūlā, 993: A Jewish woman accused two Muslims (names provided) of rape and cruel beating.

349 (c) 4 Rabīʻ al-Thānī, 993: A Muslim officer (*zaʻīm*) accused the Jew Mā'īr b. Ibrāhīm of unlawful possession of an elaborate sword. The Jew admitted having received the sword, along with a few other items, from the servant of the above-mentioned as security for a loan of 100 gold coins.

449 (f) 11 Sha'bān, 993: The Jew Ḥasān b. Saʻāda rented a room in a house that belonged to the Jew Mūsā b. Ibrāhīm for a full year for 30 silver coins.

505 (a) 26 Ramaḍān, 993: The body of the Jew Yaʻqūb b. Mūsā was found in one of the water pits in the Temple Mount, near the *maghāriba* Mosque. The district governor himself came to court in order to investigate the case. Muslim dignitaries accused the Jewish community of his death, but the community denied the allegation.

515 (e) 25 Shawwāl, 993: A similar description of the above-mentioned case.

Volume 66
(1585 - 1587)

7 (b) The first third (*awā'il*) of Dhū'l-Ḥijja, 993: A detailed description of the belongings of the deceased Ya'qūb b. Yāsif b. 'Abd al-Karīm, a spice dealer found dead in a water pit, including the value of the belongings and the various expenses incurred after his death.

9 (c) 1 Muḥarram, 994: A soap factory that belongs to a Muslim merchant is located in the Jewish quarter.

13 (b) 13 Muḥarram, 994: A request by the Armenian community to hew a new entrance to their monastery, outside the walled city near the gate located in the Jewish quarter.

176 (f) 2 Jumādā'l-'Ūlā, 994: 11 Jewish shoe-makers (names provided) came to the court and requested that Sāsī b. Shū'a be appointed head of their guild.

278 (g) 14 Shawwāl, 994: A large group of Jewish men (names provided) and women complained in court of the behaviour of a certain archer (*qawwās*) who molests them and exacts unlawful fines from them. When the kadi invited him to the court he refused to come.

286 (a) 18 Shawwāl, 994: The above-mentioned soldier finally arrived in court, and when accused by the above-mentioned Jews he swore to refrain from wrong-doing in the future.

296 (c) 2 Dhū'l-Qa'da, 994: A Moroccan Jew wearing his phylacteries in public was punished although he claimed that this was permitted in his country.

299 (a) 28 Shawwāl, 994: The Jew Mūsā b. Yahūdā the saddle-maker applied for a permit to have his house in the Jewish quarter repaired. The kadi had the building inspected, then authorized the repairs.

331 (e) 4 Dhū'l-Ḥijja, 994: The close proximity of the Nahmanides Synagogue and the neighboring mosque creates further friction and generates attempts to limit Jewish presence there.

378 (c) The last third (*awākhir*) of Muḥarram, 995: In the wake of the death of a Jewish woman, her brother and her widowed husband mutually agree on the financial terms of her inheritance.

440 (a) The last third (*awākhir*) of Ṣafar, 995: Most of the shops that were leased in the spice dealers' market were leased to Jews (names provided). Their income is part of the endowment of The Dome of the Rock. The lease is for 9 years.

466 (b) The first third (*awā'il*) of Jumādā'l-'Ūlā, 995: Yūsif b. 'Abd al-Karīm and a group of Jews came to the court to complain of the lack of meat. They produced official documents authorizing them to slaughter only on Mondays and Thursdays even when there is scarcity of meat. The kadi announced once again that they may slaughter on these days.

480 (c) The last third (*awākhir*) of Jumādā'l-'Ūlā, 995: The Jewish Samsūm asked for permission to reconstruct the complex (*ḥawsh*) in which he lives in the Jewish quarter. Permission was granted.

494 (c) The first third (*awā'il*) of Jumādā'l-Thānī, 995: The Jewish community was forced to purchase a consignment of iron which the head of the community distributed among its members. The Jew Mūsā b. Ibrāhīm asked the court to exempt him because of lack of funds and the disappearance of his son. His request was granted.

531 (i) The second third (*awāsiṭ*) of Rajab, 995: The heads of the community, Yūsif b. 'Abd al-Karīm and Mūsā b. Rammūn (?) paid the poll tax due from their community for the year 995.

563 (d) The last third (*awākhir*) of Sha'bān, 995: Several Christian silversmiths and the Jewish silversmith Ya'qūb requested explicit permission to conduct their

work at the customers' lodgings or in the markets without any particular time limit, as per their old routine.

632 (c) 4 Dhū'l-Ḥijja, 995: A Jewish merchant was found guilty of using faulty weights for the sale of grapes.

Volume 67
(1588)

151 (b) 5 Jumādā'l-'Ūlā, 996: The Jew Samsūm b. Shmū'īl reported to the kadi that parts of the hostel (*ribāṭ*) where he lived (assigned to the very poor Jews, *ṣa'ālīk*) has deteriorated and needs repairing. His request was found valid and permission was granted.

159 (a) 11 Jumādā'l-'Ūlā, 996: The exacerbated conflicts between Jews and Muslims in their adjoining places of worship–the Nahmanides Synagogue and the al-'Umarī Mosque–brought about an explicit order by the kadi banning any further use of the synagogue by the Jews.

222 (d) 1 Rajab, 996: 17 Jews (names provided) owe 460 gold coins to the endowment of Khudāwirdī Bey. The 60 coins added to the original 400 are interest for one year, transparently camouflaged as payment for a commercial transaction.

248 (d) 14 Rajab, 996: The *ṣūbāshī* ordered the inhabitants of al-Sharaf quarter to choose someone among themselves for the position of head (*shaykh*) of the neighborhood, a position which had been vacant for 20 years.

311 (b) 23 Sha'bān, 996: The head of the Jewish community Shamīla b. Yahūdā guaranteed a Jewish couple involved in a legal dispute.

449 (c) 24 Muḥarram, 997: A Christian soap-maker (*ṣabbān*) and a Jewish spice dealer agreed to exchange their respective shops in the spice dealers' market for the same sum of money (60 gold coins each) they originally undertook to pay the Temple Mount endowment.

Volume 69
(1589 - 1590)

82 (a) 22 Ṣafar, 997: The head of the Jewish community, Shamīla b. Abū Jūkār, undertook to treat all members of the community, rich or poor, equally (paying special attention to the latter) with respect to the distribution of taxes and other impositions.

143 (c) 28 Jumādā'l-'Ūlā, 997: Several Jews (names provided) complained of the misconduct of a certain Muḥammad the deputy (*nā'ib*) judge who keeps harassing them, conveys derogatory reports to the *ṣūbashī* and extorts money from them. The kadi ruled that he be arrested.

143 (d) 28 Jumādā'l-'Ūlā, 997: As the court ushers were taking the above-mentioned into custody they were accosted by several armed soldiers who set him free.

148 (e) 14 Jumādā'l-'Ūlā, 997: A detailed complaint about the misbehavior of the governor's soldiers who "plunder the Muslims, the Jews and the Christians."

189 (c) The first third (*awā'il*) of Rajab, 997: The Jewess Stīr b. Dā'ūd complained about her husband Yahūdā b. Shamīla who refused to give back a gold chain weighing 24 *mithqāl* which she had lent him.

214 (b) 24 Sha'bān, 997: A long list of Jews (names provided) who owe the endowment of Abū Sayfayn 400 *ghirsh* plus another 60, the latter allegedly for a piece of cloth they purchased, but actually as the interest on the above sum for a period of one year.

259 (c) 2 Dhū'l-Qa'da, 997: The Jew Shamsūm requested permission to have the building of the hostel (*ribāṭ*) for the Jewish poor repaired now that its roof had collapsed. The request was granted.

288 (a) 28 Dhū'l-Qa'da, 997: The Jew Yāsif b. Sha'bān accused the head (*shaykh*) of the village Na'līn of being in his

debt for 3 *qinṭār* and 60 *raṭl* of olive oil as part of their taxes due for the year 993, which had been transferred to him by the administrator (*mutawallī*) of Khasseki Sultan endowment.

288 (f) 9 Shawwāl, 997: The Jew Yāsif b. Sha'bān accused a Muslim of owing him 4 gold coins for a consignment of sugar-cane.

424 (d) 11 Muḥarram, 998: A Christian had rented a shop in the Jewish quarter, then let it to a Muslim for one year.

424 (e) 11 Muḥarram, 998: Another shop that had been leased by a Jewish tailor was now rented by the same Christian for a year.

475 (h) 7 Rabī' al-Awwal, 998: After a burglary occurred in the Jewish quarter, two Muslim suspects (one of them a butcher) were brought in for investigation, but Muslim and Jewish inhabitants attested to their spotless records.

Volume 71
(1587 - 1590)

31[89] (b) The last third (*awākhir*) of Dhū'l-Qa'da, 995: The Jewish community of Jerusalem has been conducting their services at an old synagogue adjacent to a mosque. Although earlier permits exist, entitling the Jews to worship God in their synagogue, the local governors prohibited it, thus causing the Jews to consider leaving Jerusalem altogether. The Sultan decreed that the kadi of Jerusalem should attend to the needs of the Jews, and report to Istanbul any further misconduct of this kind.

80[90] (a) [No date mentioned, end of 998.] The Jewish community of Jerusalem has been using a *waqf* plot of land called al-Jismāniyya near Jerusalem to bury their dead. They have been leasing this plot ever since the end of the 15th century for a certain fee, and recently the administrators of the al-Ṣalāḥiyya endowment insisted that they pay a substantial increase. A detailed investigation followed, and finally the local court issued a ruling finalizing the amount that the Jews would pay anually to the endowment and to the governor for the continued use of that cemetery.

---

[89] Turkish.
[90] Turkish.

Volume 72
(1590 - 1591)

97 (b) 27 Ramaḍān, 998: The heads of the Jewish community paid the poll tax due from their community to the amount of 60 units (*khāne*) and were given a receipt (*raj'a*) of acquittance by the tax collector.

263 (b) The last third (*awākhir*) of Jumādā'l-'Ūlā, 999: The head of the Jewish community, Yūsif b. 'Abd al-Karīm, came to court with the Jewish slaughterer and other Jews. There they introduced a legal opinion (*fatwā*) and a decree authorizing them to slaughter in accordance with their customs and had it recorded in the court's proceedings.

263 (c) 10 Jumādā'l-'Ūlā, 999: A large group of spice dealers (*'aṭṭār*) made up of Muslims, Jews and Christians (names provided) complained of ongoing attempts on behalf of the governors to force them to provide iron without payment. The kadi issued a ruling containing a general obligation to refrain from any further demands of this kind since, among other things, supplying iron should fall within the purview of the blacksmiths (*ḥaddād*).

264 (a) The first third (*awā'il*) of Jumādā'l-'Ūlā, 999: The heads of the Jewish community, Yūsif b. 'Abd al-Karīm and Ya'qūb, paid the tax collector the poll tax due from 84 members of their community.

305 (h) 11 Rajab, 999: A Muslim claimed in court that the Jew Abrahām b. Shmū'īl owed him 80 gold coins (at the exchange rate of 98 Mar'ash silver coins for each gold coin) for a consignment of soap. The accused acknowledged owing 75 gold coins on a *Mashriqī* silver coins basis then they agreed on 85 gold coins on the latter basis.

305 (j) 1 Muḥarram, 999: The *muftī* let his home located in the al-Rīsha quarter to the Jewish cloth merchant Yūsif b.

Sha‘bān for three years at the rate of 10 gold coins per annum.

367 (a) 11 Sha‘bān, 999: The Muslim head of the Jewish quarter reported that he had been hit over the head when, in the middle of the night, he heard the voice of a Jewish person trying to stop a thief and wanted to see for himself what was happening. He was spending the night in that neighborhood to protect it against burglary attempts and was actually hit by the chief night-watchman.

Volume 75
(1592 - 1593)

29 (c) 7 Rabīʿ al-Thānī, 1000: A group of Christian and Jewish spice dealers (names provided) came to the court and undertook in the presence of the governor's representative to purchase jointly any iron consignment that was brought to town. They equally undertook to supply the governor, or anyone else who wished to buy, with half of the demand, the other half to be provided by the blacksmiths (*ḥaddād*).

42 (c) 11 Jumādā'l-Awwal, 1000: The heads of the Jewish community, Māʾīr b. Ibrāhīm and Yūsif b. Shaʿbān, complained that when members of the community try to have their houses repaired they are asked to pay a fine. Since this procedure contravenes an explicit decree issued a year before, they asked the kadi to have the said decree registered in the court register.

49 (d) 20 Jumādā'l-'Ūlā, 1000: Christian and Jewish silversmiths (names provided) came to the court in order to complain about the high-handed behavior of the head of their guild. They requested that the latter, a Muslim, be replaced by a Jewish member of the guild. Thereupon the kadi had the Muslim head of the guild resign and appointed the Jew Arṣlān in his stead.

74 (e) 12 Rajab, 1000: Several Jews, including the Jewish slaughterer, requested that the kadi reiterate their right –based upon earlier decrees which they produced –to slaughter whenever they wished. Their request was granted.

107 (g) 2 Ramaḍān, 1000: Upon the request of two silversmiths, one of whom was the Jew ʿAbd al-Raḥīm, the kadi ruled that members of this guild may perform their work wherever they wish without any interference.

147 (k) 1 Rabīʿ al-Awwal, 1000: The kadi announced that Yūsif b. Yahūdā will slaughter according to the old custom and in the service of qualified butchers only.

180 (d) The first third (*awā'il*) of Rabīʿ al-Awwal, 1000: The expert (*'usta*) Shams b. ʿAlī b. Khālid introduced in court a document (*berāt*) announcing his nomination as head of the silversmiths' guild. He came accompanied by several Christian and eight Jewish silversmiths (names provided) who expressed their full satisfaction with him. Thereupon he was declared head of the guild.

199 (i) 26 Rajab, 1000: Several religious dignitaries (*ʿulamā'*) who subscribe to the Shāfiʿī school complained about the Jewish habit of selling to the Muslim customers those parts of their slaughtered sheep that are unfit for Jewish use. The kadi ruled that if that happens the Jewish slaughterers should stamp the meat properly to indicate its origin, then sell it only in the Jewish quarter.

223 (d) 6 Jumādā'l-Thānī, 1001: The head of the Jewish community, Sāsī b. Faraj Allah, along with several other Jews, demanded that the Jew Shmū'īl b. ʿAṭā' Allah, originally from Safed, be expelled from Jerusalem and sent back to his own town. He was given a postponement of one month to attend to his business, after which he promised to leave and return home.

229 (d) 5 Jumādā'l-Thānī, 1001: The income from the loads of soap exported from Jerusalem was leased by two business partners, a Muslim and the Jew Yūsif b. Shaʿbān, for the sum of 140 gold coins per year.

242 (c) The last third (*awākhir*) of Jumādā'l-Thānī, 1001: The Jewish and Christian silversmiths (names provided) agreed upon the price of pure silver and that of second-rate silver. They also agreed to regulate purchases and sales of their work within the guild.

276 (e) 1 Muḥarram, 1001: The silversmiths' guild members were warned to refrain from the use of counterfeit silver. However, a Muslim customer complained that she bought a pair of silver bracelets made by the Jewish silversmith Sulaymān b. Sulaymān, and they turned out

to be counterfeit silver. The above-mentioned culprit admitted his transgression and was punished.

283 (a) 10 Muḥarram, 1001: The Jew Darāhimal (?) b. Shiḥāda acknowledged his debt to a Muslim functionary.

283 (d) 10 Muḥarram, 1001: The head of the Jewish community, Shamīla b. Yahūdā, admitted that he owed a Muslim the sum of 18 gold coins and undertook to pay his debt.

318 (e) 25 Rabīʿ al-Thānī, 1001: The kadi nominated the Jew Saʿāda b. Isḥāq as a slaughterer for the Jewish community to replace the deceased Yūsif b. Yahūdā.

371 (a) 5 Dhū'l-Qaʿda, 1001: A Muslim claimed to have purchased half a house in al-Rīsha quarter from the Jewess Stīr b. Dā'ūd for 5 gold coins. The Jew Shamīla b. Yahūdā declared that his above-mentioned step-mother had sold property that did not rightly belong to her. When two Muslim witnesses testified that he inherited it from his deceased father, the kadi ruled in his favor.

387 (d) End of Shaʿbān, 1001: The kadi ruled that the Jewish slaughterers should slaughter only twice a week, on Mondays and on Fridays.

Volume 76
(1594 - 1595)

21 (f) 20 Rabīʿ al-Ākhir, 1002: The kadi warned the head of the Jewish community to refrain from having meat slaughtered by the Jewish slaughterer on any day other than Monday and Thursday.

67 (g) 27 Jumādā'l-Ākhira, 1002: Upon the death of the Jew Salamūn the kadi appointed the Jew Yūsif b. Ibrāhīm to replace him as official money changer (*ṣarrāf*) in Jerusalem for gold, silver and *ghirsh* coins.

87 (c) 5 Shaʿbān, 1002: The Jew Yahūdā b. Mūsā the blacksmith (*ḥaddād*) died in Jerusalem and his inheritance was divided among his two wives and three children (names provided).

103 (f) 7 Ramaḍān, 1002: The Jew Furaykh (?) b. Yūsif had left Jerusalem for a long period without providing his wife with any means of subsistence. Upon her request the kadi ruled that she is entitled to up to one silver coin per day for her *nafaqa* basic needs which she may use out of her husband's property.

113 (b) 23 Ramaḍān, 1002: The heads of the Jewish community paid the poll tax due from the members of their community in the amount of 80 tax units (*khāne*) to the endowment of the Temple Mount and 60 "units" to the Imperial Treasury (*al-khāṣṣ al-sharīf*).

113 (d) 20 Ramaḍān, 1002: The Jew Abrāhām b. Mūsā b. Ramūn acknowledged that he owed a Muslim a debt of 321 gold coins for a consignment of soap.

115 (b) 4 Shawwāl, 1002: The Jew Abrāhām b. Sālim admitted that he owed Ibrāhīm b. Shmū'īl the convert (*al-muhtadī*) 50 gold coins.

131 (i) 27 Rajab, 1002: The Jew Yūsif b. Shaʿbān claimed that he was entitled to six months' pay in his capacity as

money changer (*ṣayrafī*) of the Khasseki Sultan endowment. Upon investigation of the case the kadi authorized this payment.

184 (b) 11 Dhū'l-Qa'da, 1002: Several prominent Jews requested that the kadi sanction the expulsion of the convert Ibrāhīm b. Shmū'īl from the Jewish quarter. When the kadi established that his presence there was a cause of friction he ordered him to leave the Jewish quarter and find himself lodgings in "one of the Muslim neighborhoods."

184 (c) 11 Dhū'l-Qa'da, 1002: The above-mentioned Jews leased the above-mentioned convert's house for three years he let it to them for 4 gold coins per year.

201 (b) 9 Dhū'l-Qa'da, 1002: The Jew Karsūn living in Istanbul transferred the debt of 20,000 silver coins (*'uthmānī*) that the kadi of al-Madina owed him for a consignment of cloth as well as a loan, to the Jewish cloth merchant Yūsif b. Sha'bān and Mā'īr b. Abrāhām in Jerusalem. Upon receipt of the funds they delivered a pre-signed receipt written by Karsūn to the kadi.

206 (c) 19 Dhū'l-Ḥijja, 1002: A group of Jewish dignitaries guaranteed the debt of 300 gold coins owed by another group of Jews (names provided) to the Muslim head of the merchants' guild (*shaykh al-tujjār*). Another 80 gold coins are presented as a separate debt incurred as a result of a cloth sale, which is the regular formulation indicating the interest due.

206 (d) 19 Dhū'l-Ḥijja, 1002: The Jewish cloth merchant Mā'īr b. Abrāhām incurred a separate debt of 240 gold coins to the head of the merchants' guild. The principal was 200, and the interest (presented as a sale) was 40 gold coins.

215 (a) 26 Dhū'l-Ḥijja, 1002: Two Jewish converts testified that they knew the Jew Sa'āda b. Isḥāq and knew he was an Israelite (*isrā'īlī*), that both he and his father practised slaughtering. Thereupon the kadi authorized Sa'āda to slaughter for his community.

226 (d) 1 Muḥarram, 1003: A Jewish silversmith denied the accusation of a Muslim tailor that he owed him 24 *dirham* of silver.

226 (e) 1 Muḥarram, 1003: A Muslim merchant claimed that he was entitled to 100 gold coins from the Jew Mūsā b. Yahūdā the saddle-maker both as a debtor and as a guarantor for several other Jewish debtors (names provided).

226 (h) 1 Muḥarram, 1003: A Muslim claimed that the Jew Ya'qūb b. Sālim and 'Abbūd b. 'Abd al-Karīm owed him 5 gold coins.

294 (c) 3 Jumādā'l-'Ūlā, 1003: The Jewish Mā'īr b. Abrāhām bought 135 *mudd* of wheat from the former governor of the Jerusalem district for 67.5 gold coins.

331 (a) The first third (*awā'il*) of Jumādā'l-'Ūlā, 1003: The inventory of the properties of a deceased Egyptian *shaykh* indicates a debt of 13 gold coins incurred by a Jewish shoe-maker.

331 (f) 3 Rabī' al-Thānī, 1003: A Jew converted to Islam leased a mill in the Jewish quarter for a year and a half.

376 (d) The first third (*awā'il*) of Rajab, 1003: A group of Jews (names provided) requested that the kadi register in his *sijill* proceedings an earlier imperial decree to the effect that no one may harass those Jews who convene in a private house for prayer and worship of God as long as there are no "pictures" or any fixture resembling the direction of prayer (*miḥrāb*, the Muslim equivalent of the Jewish *mizraḥ*).

434 (d) The last third (*awākhir*) of Sha'bān, 1003: The heads of the Jewish community paid the poll tax due from their community for the year 1003.

448 (j) 16 Rajab, 1003: The Jew Abrāhām b. 'Āmrān and Mā'īr b. Abrāhām owe the endowment of Khudāwirdī Bey otherwise known as Abū Sayfayn, 40 gold coins and another 6 gold coins in return for a pair of bracelets (i.e. hidden interest).

479 (b) The last third (*awākhir*) of Ramaḍān, 1003: Several Jewish dignitaries (names provided) declared that they release the Jews Ibrāhīm b. Ḥayyin al-Kūhīn, 'Ifrāyim b. Yahūdā and Mā'īr b. Shmū'īl from any further responsibility for Jewish debts to Muslims.

540 (a) 27 Dhū'l-Qa'da, 1003: When the debt of 20,000 silver coins to Karsūn, the Jewish rabbi (*khakhām*) from Istanbul was settled (cf. above, *sijill* 76/201 (b)), a group of Jewish dignitaries came to the court and declared that the above-mentioned sum was distributed among the poor of the Jewish community of Jerusalem.

Volume 77
(1595 - 1596)

11	(c)	17 Shawwāl, 1003: Members of the Jewish community asked the kadi to appoint Mūsā b. Sālim b. Murdakhāy as their spokesman (*mutakallim*) (last part illegible).
86	(b)	25 Muḥarram, 1004: "Many" Jews came to the court and asked the kadi to appoint Ya'qūb b. Barūkh as the scribe (*kātib*) of the community, and Sāsī b. Faraj-Allah as the head (*shaykh*) of the community. They all undertook to obey unconditionally everything they say and do.
96	(c)	7 Muḥarram, 1004: The Jew Ya'qūb b. Mūsā claimed that the Jew Khalīfa b. Shiḥāta owed him 10 gold coins for a commercial transaction. The above-mentioned Ya'qūb and Sāsī gave testimony in support of the plaintiff and the kadi ruled in his favor.
96	(d)	7 Muḥarram, 1004: The above-mentioned Khalīfa claimed that the above-mentioned Ya'qūb owed him 30 *mudd* wheat and 15 *mudd* barley he had given him as a deposit (*wadī'a*).
107	(c)	24 Muḥarram, 1004: A Muslim merchant demanded payment of a debt of 50 gold coins from the Jew Ya'qūb b. Barūkh who had guaranteed the Jewish community for it.
107	(i)	24 Muḥarram, 1004: The Jew Sāsūn b. Mūsā admitted owing 3.5 gold coins to a Muslim.
134	(b)	5 Rabī' al-Awwal, 1004: The Jew Shamīla b. Yahūdā b. 'Abd al-Karīm purchased from his brothers for 7.5 gold coins another part of the house they all inherited and owned.
149		17 Rabī' al-Awwal, 1004: A very detailed document summing up the earlier stages and different considerations in the legal dispute that led to the closure

of the Nahmanides Synagogue. The kadi postponed his verdict as to whether it should be turned into a mosque or returned to Jewish hands pending receipt of the document that may prove the rights of the Jewish community to acquire the building.

162 (a) 14 Ṣafar, 1004: The Jewish saddle-maker Shūba b. Mūsā guaranteed the Jewish woman Kalāla b. Ibrāhīm for debts she may incur in conjunction with her function as a public-crier (*dallāla*).

162 (b) 14 Ṣafar, 1004: The Jewess Marḥaba b. Mūsā guaranteed another Jewish woman, Simḥa b. Yūsif the public-crier, and Simḥa guaranteed Marḥaba. Both women were guaranteed by Ḥasan, the Muslim public-crier.

162 (c) 14 Ṣafar, 1004: The kadi warned the Jewish woman Ḥannā b. Shūba not to work as public-crier, nor should she in this capacity take anything for public sale unless she has a formal guarantor (*kafīl*).

163 (f) 18 Ṣafar, 1004: Several Jewish dignitaries (names provided) reported the death of Biṣālīl their rabbi, adding that from now on they are in no need of a rabbi (*khākhām*). Should there be an issue concerning the governor that the rabbi would have dealt with in the past, they will have their deputy (*nā'ib*) attend to it.

298 (e) 4 Rajab, 1004: Several Jewish dignitaries (names provided) owe the Khudāwirdī Bey endowment 40 gold coins as well as an additional sum (i.e. interest on the principal) of 6 gold coins in return for a pair of bracelets they bought.

345 (c) 8 Ramaḍān, 1004: At the request of the kadi, five Jewish dignitaries (names provided) guarantee the debt of the Jewish community to the amount of 100 gold coins.

358 (d) The first third (*awā'il*) of Ramaḍān, 1004: The head of the Jewish community, Sāsī b. Faraj-Allah, paid the tax collector the poll tax due for the year 1004 from the Jewish community.

387 (c) 10 Shawwāl, 1004: Seven distinguished Jews came to the court and complained about the refusal of another Jew, Mūsā b. Ibrāhīm, to share with them the burden of debts they had incurred for the general use of the community and for payment of taxes. The kadi ruled in their favor, based on their testimony as well as the evidence of Muslim witnesses to the effect that although the dignitaries of the community personally undertake to pay, the actual payments are shared equally by all members of the community.

476 (a) 21 Muḥarram, 1005: The highest financial authority (*defterdār*) of Damascus sent a special envoy to collect the poll tax due from the Jews and Christians of Jerusalem for 1005. The rate was higher for the Jews (107 silver coins per person) than for the Christians (82).

501 (g) 13 Ṣafar, 1005: The kadi leased the income of *bayt al-māl* of the Jews to the Jews Mā'īr b. Abrāhām, Yūsif b. Sha'bān and Ya'qūb b. Barūkh for the sum of 25 gold coins per year.

512 (i) 27 Rabī' al-Awwal, 1005: After closure of the Nahmanides Synagogue 40 Torah scrolls were taken out and deposited for safe-keeping in a sealed room. Four of these were now stolen by several Jews (names provided) who claimed that they belonged to them.

521 (c) The first third (*awā'il*) of Rabī' al-Thānī, 1005: The dignitaries of the Jewish community (names provided) confirmed receipt of 510 *ghirsh* brought from Venice by the Damascene Jew Yahūdā b. Mūsā alias Mish'ān.

565-569 The first third (*awā'il*) of Rajab, 1003: A very long and detailed list of all the different shops leased out by the al-Aqṣā Mosque endowment in the various markets of Jerusalem. Many Jewish names among them.

Volume 78
(1596 - 1598)

11 (a) The second third (*awāsiṭ*) of Rabīʿ al-Awwal, 1005: The heads of the Jewish community remitted the additional payments of the poll tax due from their community for 1005.

66 (b) 2 Rajab, 1005: The heads of the community paid the annual sum of 46 gold coins due to the Abū Sayfayn endowment.

87 (d) 27 Rajab, 1005: The kadi imposed on a Muslim expert (*'usta*) the payment of 36 *pāra*[91] he owed a Jewish cloth merchant for an earlier purchase of cloth.

88 (j) 1 Shaʿbān, 1005: A Muslim owes the Jewish cloth merchant Yūsif b. Shaʿbān 7 gold coins for a sale of several kinds of cloth.

89 (c) 2 Shaʿbān, 1005: The Jewish cloth merchant Yūsif b. Shaʿbān claimed that the Muslim head of the merchants owed him 17 gold coins for a variety of pieces of silk, cotton and wool cloth.

97 (h) 7 Shaʿbān, 1005: The Jewish cloth merchant Yūsif b. Shaʿbān demanded that a Muslim pay his debt for cotton cloth (*quṭayna*) he had purchased from him.

127 (a) 3 Ramaḍān, 1005: Several prominent Jews (names provided, including their rabbi) could not pay the accumulated debts of the entire community amounting to 5,000 *ghirsh*. Thereupon they were arrested and imprisoned together with many Muslims. They requested to be transferred to a separate building nearby where they could keep their Sabbath, refrain from constituting a cause for friction with the other inmates,

---

[91] One *pāra* was the equivalent of two *'uthmānī* or one fortieth of the *sulṭānī* gold coin; *EI*, s.v. "Pāra."

but still be in official custody. Their request was granted.

149 (b) 4 Ramaḍān, 1005: The Jew Ya'qūb b. Yūsif admitted that he owed the Jew Isḥāq al-'Arīnī (?) the sum of 2 *ghirsh* for his lodging in the Jewish quarter.

149 (d) 5 Ramaḍān, 1005: Seven prominent Jews (names provided) acknowledged a debt of 135 gold coins for which they undertook to pay 10 immediately.

196 (e) 1 Shawwāl, 1005: The Jew 'Āzir b. Sha'bān left for Egypt and authorized the Jew Ya'qūb b. Yūsif to lend his wife any sum of money she needed during his absence. Having spent the total of 15 gold coins Ya'qūb now demanded to be reimbursed.

247 (b) 21 Dhū'l-Ḥijja, 1005: The Jew Kalsūn, the rabbi of the Jewish community of Istanbul, sent a sum of 10,000 silver coins to Mā'īr b. Abrāhām and the other dignitaries (*kubarā'*) of the Jewish community of Jerusalem to be distributed to the poor of the community. The above-mentioned Mā'īr reported that he had concluded the distribution of the above sum.

485 (c) 27 Rabī' al-Thānī, 1006: A Muslim clerk in al-Aqṣā Mosque claimed that Isḥāq al-'Uraynī, Ya'qūb b. Bārūkh and Ya'qūb b. Barūz owed him 345 gold coins both as guarantors and as debtors. They acknowledged the debt and agreed to pay 45 gold coins on account.

Volume 79
(1598 - 1599)

43 (h) 3 Rajab, 1006: The heads of the Jewish community owe the Abū Sayfayn endowment the sum of 46 gold coins.

119 (b) 18 Ramaḍān, 1006: A Muslim butcher claimed that the Jewish shoe-maker Shiḥāda b. Mūsā had bought hides from him for the sum of 12 gold coins. When two Muslim witnesses testified that the actual debt was 10 gold coins the kadi ruled that this sum be paid to the plaintiff.

119 (c) 18 Ramaḍān, 1006: The same Muslim butcher demanded from another Jewish butcher, Sulaymān b. Manṣūr, 5 gold coins and 10 silver coins for a consignment of hides he had purchased from his father. The butcher claimed that his debt amounted to 4 gold coins and 30 silver coins the kadi ruled that he pay the latter sum.

134 (c) 4 Shawwāl, 1006: The Moroccan Jew Yūsif b. Shmū'īl accused a convert to Islam (*muhtadī*) of having beaten him. The defendant argued that his wife, now converted to Islam, had been the plaintiff's spouse and he cursed her publicly, which brought about the immediate fray. Upon the testimony of two Jews the defendant was convicted.

235 (a) 25 Dhū'l-Ḥijja, 1006: Seven distinguished Jews came to the court and requested that the kadi appoint Ya'qūb b. Bārūkh *al-ḥāmī* as head of the community, to be in charge of collection of their taxes as well as of expenditures on matters that pertain to the community.

396 (a) The second third (*awāsiṭ)* of Jumādā'l-'Ūlā, 1007: The Moroccan Jew Isḥāq b. Murdakhāy requested the kadi, in the presence of the head of the community, to forbid the Jewish community from imposing on him a disproportionally large share of the debts they owed. Request was granted.

438 (a) The second third (*awāsiṭ*) of Jumādā'l-Thānī, 1007: The heads of the community describe the routine they follow when they take loans for the community as a whole and enter names of debtors even if some of those named are not present.

445 (f) 21 Jumādā'l-'Ūlā, 1007: The heads of the Jewish community acknowledge a debt of 30 gold coins to a Muslim creditor in return for a loan.

453 (f) 27 Jumādā'l-'Ūlā, 1007: The Jew Yūsif b. ʻAbd al-Karīm guaranteed 4 other Jews (names provided) for a loan.

471 (b) 10 Rajab, 1007: The heads of the Jewish community report to the kadi that they routinely enter names of other members of the community as debtors when they take loans or incur other debts for the entire community.

532 (a) 28 Shaʻbān, 1007: The heads of the Jewish community tried to force a Jewish woman, Simḥa b. Isḥāq, to pay the debts of her dead husband who had not resided in Jerusalem. She convinced the kadi to exempt her from payment of her husband's debts.

573 (a) The second third (*awāsiṭ*) of Shaʻbān, 1006: The kadi agreed to a recurrent request of the heads of the Jewish community imprisoned for unpaid community debts, to be detained henceforth in a separate building so that Muslim prisoners could not interfere with their prayers or with their keeping of the Sabbath.

Volume 80
(1599 - 1600)

13 (h) 1 Ramaḍān, 1007: A Muslim woman claimed that the head of the Jewish community along with several other Jews owed her 30 gold coins, of which they paid her only 16 *ghirsh* (most probably substituting *ghirsh* and *sulṭānī* for gold coins). They acknowledged her claim.

17 (b) The first third (*awā'il*) of Ramaḍān, 1007: A Muslim creditor demanded that the heads of the Jewish community repay him 360 gold coins he had lent them. They claimed that four years earlier they had borrowed 120 gold coins from him. The kadi consulted several legal opinions (*fatwā*) and ruled that his demand was tantamount to simply asking for interest (*ribā*) which was forbidden in Islam, hence he decided that they pay him only 120 coins.

20 (b) 5 Ramaḍān, 1007: A Jewish undertaker would not let another Jew bury his sister-in-law unless he paid 12 gold coins. When other Jews testified (names provided) that this was not an authorized payment, the kadi ruled against the undertaker and had him flogged.

20 (c) 7 Ramaḍān, 1007: The kadi personally visited the Jewish quarter to verify allegations that the Jews pray loudly there. He entered a house where both men and women were praying at the top of their voices. Their answer to his query was that the house had been turned into a synagogue.

28 (b) 7 Ramaḍān, 1007: On a Sabbath the kadi went to the Jewish quarter and entered a house where they were worshipping God. He inquired as to the nature of this house and was shown an imperial decree authorizing the use of private houses as synagogues provided that no permanent religious fixtures were installed.

31 (a) 23 Ramaḍān, 1007: Attempts by the religious authorities of al-Ṣalāḥiyya endowment to raise the rent for the Jewish cemetery in Gethsemane.

40 (d) 6 Shawwāl, 1007: The kadi appointed Abrāhām b. 'Amrān as rabbi (*khākhām*) for the Jewish community.

74 (h) The last third (*awākhir*) of Shawwāl, 1007: The Muslim merchant Badr al-Dīn purchased several pieces of real estate: a room and a kitchen from the Jewish woman Qamrā b. Yahūdā the rabbi "in the Jewish quarter (*maḥalla*) within al-Rīsha quarter (*maḥalla)*" for 29 gold coins; a room and two kitchens in the above-mentioned house from the Jewish woman Simḥa b. Mūsā for 9 gold coins; an upper floor and one room on the lower floor in the same building from the Jew Abrāhām b. Yahūdā for 10 gold coins.

190 (b) 24 Ṣafar, 1008: The Jew Mūsā b. Abrāhām, originally from Istanbul, now residing in Jerusalem, appointed a soldier stationed in the Citadel of Jerusalem to use all possible legal means in order to have another Jew, who lived in Safed, pay his debt of 40 gold coins.

190 (c) 20 Muḥarram, 1008: The above-mentioned Jew also asked the above-mentioned soldier to collect another debt of 25 gold coins in Safed.

336 (a) 17 Rajab, 1008: The heads of the community declare the Jew Mā'īr b. Isḥāq not liable for any debts or obligations to the community.

344 (a) 25 Rajab, 1008: As a result of Muslim attempts to stop Jewish pilgrims from visiting Nabī Shmū'īl so that only Muslims might visit the shrine, an imperial decree was issued–in response to a Jewish petition–forbidding any disruption or impeding of Jewish pilgrimage to the shrine.

555 (b) 20 Muḥarram, 1008: A detailed inventory of the legacy left by the deceased Rabbi Efrāyim.

Volume 82
(1600 - 1601)

51 (b) 15 Ṣafar, 1009: The Moroccan rabbi Ya'qūb b. Abrāhām recounted that he had come to Jerusalem for a pilgrimage and stayed until the Holiday of Succoth (*'īd al-'arsh*). The heads of the community then tried to involve him in the payment of their debts even though he was a foreigner there. The kadi ruled that he be exempted.

57 (c) 19 Ṣafar, 1009: Similarly, the Jew Mā'īr b. Shmū'īl recounted an identical problem, except that in his case the community also made him their rabbi. He also requested of the kadi that he be exempted from any debt of the community. His request was granted.

82 (c) The second third (*awāsiṭ*) of Ṣafar, 1009: The heads (*ru'asā*) of the Jewish community paid the poll tax due for 84 people (*nafar*) to The Dome of the Rock's endowment for the year 1009.

136 (c) 15 Rabī' al-Thānī, 1009: A shop located in "the Jewish market" (*sūq al-yahūd*) was leased by the two *'imāms* of The Dome of the Rock to a third Muslim for one year.

136 (h) 15 Rabī' al-Thānī, 1009: The kadi granted the dignitaries of the Jewish community their request to appoint Ibrāhīm b. Mūsā the saddle-maker as their head.

274 (b) 15 Ramaḍān, 1009: The Jewish saddle-maker Ibrāhīm b. Mūsā complained that the head of the community wanted him to share the financial burdens of the wheat-merchants (*ḥaddār*) and therefore declared him a wheat-merchant. He asked the kadi to pronounce him a shoe-maker, as testified by two Jewish witnesses, and his request was granted.

339 (a) 14 Dhū'l-Qa'da, 1009: The heads of the community complained that they were being harassed by Muslims

who would not let them slaughter, although they have imperial authorization to do so. The kadi inspected their documents, then gave them permission to slaughter whenever there is meat and to sell it in their neighborhood.

339 (f) 14 Dhū'l-Qaʿda, 1009: The Jew Sulaymān b. Isḥāq purchased from other Jews (names provided) a house in the Jewish quarter for the sum of 20 *ghirsh.*

364 (c) 7 Dhū'l-Ḥijja, 1009: The Karaite physician renewed the lease from the Muslim comptroller of the Aḥmad al-Thawrī endowment for a plot of land for thirty years, which he may use for a variety of purposes, including the burial of members of his community. Location and measurements are provided.

368 (a) 10 Dhū'l-Ḥijja, 1009: A Muslim purchased 2 rooms for the sum of 11 gold coins in a house that belonged to Jewish people in the Jewish quarter.

INDEX[92]

92 Prepared by E. Lassman

Library of Congress Cataloging-in-Publication Data

Cohen, Amnon, 1936-
A world within: Jewish life as reflected in Muslim court documents from the Sijill of Jerusalem (XVIth century) / Amnon Cohen.
p. cm.
"The present study ... is an accumulation of most 'Jewish' cases found in the 16th-century registers"--Preface.
"A Jewish quarterly review supplement."
Includes bibliographical references and index.
Contents: pt. 1. Texts -- pt. 2. Facsimiles
1. Jews--Jerusalem--History--16th century--Sources. 2. Jews--Legal status, laws, etc.--Jerusalem--History--16th century--Sources. 3. Jerusalem--Ethnic relations--Sources. I. Jerusalem. Mehkeme-i şer'iye. Sijill. II. Jewish quarterly review (Philadelphia, Pa.) III. Title.
DS109.92.C62 1994 305.892'40569442'09031--dc20
ISBN 0-960268-68-5 (pt. 1)
ISBN 0-935135-00-6 (pt. 2)

94-43469
CIP